LETTERS FROM THE FAR SIDE OF THE SHINING SEA

by

Anne Reed McCullough

FIRST EDITION

Library of Congress Catalog Card No: 92-61998
ISBN: 1-56002-218-3

UNIVERSITY EDITIONS, Inc.
59 Oak Lane, Spring Valley
Huntington, West Virginia 25704

Cover by Lyne

D0905711

Dedication

To the wives of all World War Two servicemen but most particularly to the wives of Navy pilots because they have truly walked a mile in my shoes.

And to the many and sympathetic mail carriers of that era (We started watching for them daily hours before they were due, and when they finally appeared, we mentally strewed the sidewalk with rose petals to facilitate their approach) who walked many miles in their own shoes to bring us the only things that kept our spirits up during those long and lonesome days—letters from the far side of the shining sea.

Acknowledgments

With grateful thanks to Dave Lister and Wayne Thompson —both enlisted men serving on the flight deck of the U.S.S. Enterprise at the time she was Bob's home away from home.

To Dave because of his letters of encouragement.

To Wayne because he allowed me to make use of interesting and priceless information he recorded while it was happening.

Foreword

From 1940 through 1945 Bob wrote me some 250 letters from wherever he happened to be while serving as a Naval Aviator before and during World War II. When he came home for good, I stored the letters in a box in the attic. While he was alive I felt no need to read them, and after this death I could not read them, nor could I throw them away.

In April of this year I went to the first reunion of his squadron, VFN90. I really didn't want to go—I was afraid, as with his letters, the memories would be too painful, but I felt somehow drawn and so I went. It was a marvelous and happily nostalgic experience. Outwardly there were lots of changes— some bald heads, some medicine ball stomachs, some limps, but inside they were all the same as they had been forty-five years ago and still young at heart, and they told me so many stories about Bob that I had never known before.

After I came home it gave me the courage to break out his letters and I found the same thing to be true of them. Very strangely, while reading them it was as if I were back in time and we were living once more all those times together. Returning to the past was not as devastating as I had thought it would be, but instead brought back happy memories.

I couldn't believe how closely his letters paralleled the events as depicted in *From Sea to Shining Sea and Back Again*—depicting the events, of course from Bob's standpoint.

I have therefore correlated his letters with my writings and interwoven them into one manuscript which I believe to be the epitome of life as we lived it in those long ago years of World War II.

Chapter 1

February 1985

Back in the winters of 1945 and 1946 I whiled away the time recounting how Bob and I, and subsequently our daughter, Anne, wove our way through World War II. For some obscure reason I threw this journal into the incinerator a few years later. I've always regretted this loss, especially since I found Grandfather Reed's Civil War Journal so interesting. Although I'm now somewhat incapacitated with a broken right wrist, I thought I'd devote some time this winter, some thirty-nine years later, trying to recall the events which befell us during the war years. Perhaps I'll never finish, but anyway I shall start, urged on by Anne and Bruce who say they realize they know nothing about Bob's and my life up to the time they were able to remember.

Originally I began describing various happenings that took place just before and after Bob and I were married in October of 1939. Though we didn't realize it then, World War II began for us at 0001 hours, 1 April 1940, when the portion of the Pacific fleet based at San Diego sailed out for six weeks of war games in the Pacific. As far as I know it never returned per se until after VJ day in 1945.

It now occurs to me that before delving into the many partings and reunions that marked those hectic years, I should explain something of my own background and what I know of Bob's. I was born Anne Reed in Washington, D.C. in 1915, the product of a union between the ante-bellum South and damn Yankee Back Bay Boston, and as a result my southern indolence and my northern get-up-and-go have used my body as a dueling ground ever since—with, I'm afraid, the former winning out over the latter more often than not. This is probably why I never became the perfect New England housewife that my mother-in-law hoped her son would marry.

My father's family came to America in 1634, missing the Mayflower by about fifteen years. They settled in Chelsea, Mass., but as time went on moved along the periphery of Boston until they ended up in Hingham in the early 1900's. My father used to say the family's one claim to fame during the Revolution was that one of them hid under the bed with John Quincy Adams when the British went marching by. My mother's first ancestor to come to America was a Dr. James Wooten, who accompanied Captain John Smith when he founded Jamestown, Va. in 1607. The doctor was too smart to spend the winter in Jamestown, but lived aboard ship and treated his patients from there. Many of them died over the first winter, though I hope not from his ministrations, but probably due to the unaccustomed rigors of the climate. The Wooten family eventually ended up owning a plantation near Kinston, North Carolina, which is near Goldsborough.

My two grandfathers fought on opposite sides in the Civil War; Grandfather Reed, my father's father, enlisted for six months (as was allowed) in the G.A.R. As an enlisted man he was sent with the 44th Regiment to New Bern, North Carolina, from whence they sallied forth to destroy a certain White Horse Bridge near Kinston. My grandfather left a most interesting journal about this period of his life, and the first time I read it I was really fascinated. I knew that my southern grandfather's plantation lay along the route that the 44th Regiment took, and that at some period it was burned by the Yankees. All I could think as I read that journal was "oh dear, one grandfather is going to destroy the other one, and I'll never get to be born." Fortunately this didn't happen and here I am.

My Yankee grandfather served his six months, then returned to Boston and flourished mightily. My southern grandfather Sanderlin didn't fare so well. He lost everything he had except the plantation property itself, and after the war the family moved to Raleigh and lived in genteel poverty. This grandfather had the reputation for being something of a roue, and after fathering six daughters he departed this world, leaving my grandmother to raise them as best she could. She managed somehow, moving to Washington D.C. and bringing up her children in the best pre-Civil War tradition. Although she bore my grandfather six children, this southern lady always addressed him as "Mr. Sanderlin".

In the early 1900's it was considered unladylike for females to work outside the home. However, the sisters all had to find jobs, but as they never talked about what they did I don't know much about it; I think my mother worked as a secretary. My father was with the U.S. Forest Service, and somehow they met in Ogden, Utah, fell in love and were married. They came back to live in Washington soon after the birth of my older sister. Her name was Rosalie, but she was henceforth known to family and friends as 'Wo'.

This marriage caused consternation in both families. The southern relatives were still fighting the Civil War and held all Northerners responsible for the destruction of their way of life. The northern side thought all Southerners were brutes, who beat their male slaves indiscriminately and slept with female slaves in the same manner. Of course, generally speaking little of this was true of either side.

My sister and I had rather uneventful childhoods and were brought up in the best southern tradition. A young lady curtsies when introduced, a young lady never speaks unless spoken to, never puts her elbows on the table, always behaves decorously, and, of course, a young lady never shows her feelings. We were

8

taught to entertain and be the most gracious of hostesses, and led to believe we'd never have to clean house, cook a meal, or clean up after it. Except when I was at summer camp I never made my bed or picked up my clothes until I went off to college. O tempora, O mores—how things changed when the war years came.

By that time my sister Wo had been married to a naval aviator, Tom Blackburn, for five years. It was taken for granted that a married naval officer's household would include a maid, and we felt sorry for a young lieutenant's wife who lived nearby—two children and no maid! I was sure this couldn't happen to me. When Bob and I were first married I didn't want a maid; I wanted to show him what a good little housewife I could be. I even ironed his jockey shorts and socks, and the first time I cleaned our two-room duplex it took me three hours just to dust the furniture, dry mop the floors and carpetsweep the rug. Bob didn't even notice that I'd done this, and it ended any desire I ever had to excel in the domestic arts. In fact in all my married life I never had a maid; just the occasional cleaning lady when things got too bad.

Though I was so steeped in southern culture, I have always spoken with a modified Boston accent. I can't account for this, but remember vaguely my mother saying she liked the sound of a broad 'A', so to please her I guess I acquired it and still have it 65 years later. I was graduated from Holton-Arms in Washington when I was seventeen. This was a finishing school then, though six of us out of a class of twenty-eight went on to college; in my case, to Smith. There I spent four delightful and constructive years, and really learned a great deal, though I used to say the most practical things I learned were to smoke, to knit and to play bridge! Later I learned to appreciate the value of my education.

I spent the winter after graduation in Washington, but since I was too old to be included in coming-out parties and resulting social affairs I found life quite boring. So when my sister asked me to say with her while she awaited the birth of her first child, I agreed with alacrity. Tom was attached to the USS Lexington and they were living in Coronado, California, where the following events began.

Chapter 2

It was in August of 1937 when I went to Coronado to be with Wo, while her husband Tom was away on sea duty. Their baby was due in mid September, but there was a lot to see and to do for someone who had never been in Southern California before so time passed quickly. As for example, Caliente had not yet been closed so we all used to get gussied up on a Saturday night and go down and lose our money at the roulette or blackjack tables. Or we could go to the formal dances in the Circus Room at the Hotel Del Coronado which was really exciting because there was always a sprinkling of lesser movie stars on the dance floor. Or we could go over to San Diego to the El Cortez to ride the outside elevator to its top and there dine elegantly in a small replica of the top of the Mark. Then the El Cortez was the tallest building in town. Now it can't even be seen, and I believe is owned by one of California's zany religious sects.

Soon it was September 14. Wo, Tom and I were sitting at the lunch table (husbands always came home for lunch from the Air Station), when Wo said she thought she would have the baby that afternoon. Tom said she was nuts and went back to work. About an hour later her pains really did start to come quickly. I tried to get hold of Tom, but, of course, he was off on a flight so I left a message for him, drove her to the hospital and sat around nervously doing all the stupid things Tom should have been doing as an expectant father. Incidentally, I was Tom's stand-in at the birth of both his children, and believe me, I would rather go through labor four times than play surrogate father once.

He said later he thought we were both talking through our hats so instead of dashing over to the hospital from the Air Station, he went home, took a shower, had something to eat and meandered over to find his son was already a couple of hours old.

Wo was contentedly napping so we left deciding we should stop at a bar in Coronado to celebrate Tom's firstborn. I should explain that while it was easy to tell Wo and me apart when we were together, our features and coloring were so similar that when just one of us was there, it was difficult for an individual to figure out which of us it was. While we were sitting at the bar a friend of Wo's and Tom's whom I had never met came over, and Tom said, "Won't you have a drink with us? We are celebrating because Wo had a baby this afternoon" (this was in the era when after producing a child, the new mother was kept in bed for two weeks not even being allowed to dangle her legs over the side of the bed until the 13th day). Tom's friend did a double take with eyes almost popping out of his head until Tom explained that I was not his wife but her lookalike sister.

10

Poor Tom spent a miserable two weeks culinary-wise. The kitchen and I were completely unacquainted, and though I really tried the results were apt to be disastrous i.e., nobody told me to parboil the pepper shells and to saute the onions before stuffing the former and putting them into the oven to bake. We went out to dinner that night. My other worst disaster was a prune souffle, always a mile high and nicely browned and fluffy when someone else made it, but in my case a soggy mess about a half an inch thick.

My most perilous meal, though, was when I tried to roast a leg of lamb. Just as I turned on the gas to light the oven Tom called from the front yard where he was cleaning out the lily pond, asking for a large knife. I took it to him and hung casually around watching for a couple of minutes and then went back into the kitchen and struck a match. Can you believe any one could have been so stupid as not to have turned the gas off before leaving the kitchen? I was also extremely fortunate in that the ensuing explosion only singed off my eyelashes, eyebrows, and made my hairline recede temporarily about a half an inch.

Two years later when Bob and I announced our wedding plans my very first present was a Fannie Farmer cookbook sent anonymously. The bookstore wouldn't tell me nor would Tom even to this day admit to it, but it was just about the most useful present I got, and I still have it today dog-eared and food-stained, but I do think it helped our marriage survive.

One afternoon shortly after Wo and the baby came home from the hospital Tom took me, in Wo's place, to a cocktail party where I met for the first time the new breed in the Navy known as the Aviation Cadet (to be described later) which would determine the course my life would take. I immediately fancied myself in love with a very personable pilot with a Texas accent and all the attributes that went with it. We had a whirlwind romance for two or three months, but it was too intense and soon burned itself out. So for the next year and a half I lightheartedly played the field though I still feel a nostalgic twinge when I hear certain songs extant at that time—Dipsy Doodle, Once in a While or I Get Along Without You Very Well.

The event that stands out most in my mind during this heady period was the day we went to the S.M.U.-U.S.C. (or was it U.C.L.A.?) game. There were five of us—Annie and Gil Smith, one of the ostensibly unmarried married cadet couples, Ed Stebbins, Bill Gage (both of whom had gone to S.M.U.) and I. We were all from back east so when we left Coronado to drive up to L.A. on a cool, crisp California morning we dressed as for a football game in cold, frosty New England—warm coats, extra sweaters, scarves, hats and gloves. Of course, as the sun rose higher so did the temperature, and by the time we got to the Coliseum we had stripped to the bare essentials but were still

11

uncomfortably warm sitting all afternoon in the warm California sun.

Liquor was not allowed in the stadium, but that was easily circumvented by buying bottles of coke (no cans then), partially emptying them and filling the resultant space with rum brought along with that purpose in mind. It was an exciting game, and that plus the combination of hot sun and Cuban rum left us feeling no pain by the time S.M.U. had unexpectedly won.

The boys decided they wanted to go over to the Biltmore where the S.M.U. team was lodged as they had several friends on the team. When we got there, we found females weren't allowed on the team's floor so they just dumped Annie and me in the lobby and said they would be back in a while. It was fun at first mingling with the celebrants, but as time went on and on and on and no boys appeared, we got annoyed and then indignant. We tried to contact them but were unable to do so, so we did the only thing we could think of. The Biltmore lobby stretched for about a block from one door to the other. It was a split-level with four steps joining one section to the other. We sat down on the top step in the midst of a surging crowd and announced that we weren't moving until someone brought us back our dates. They appeared very shortly looking hacked and embarrassed and dragged us away as quickly and unobtrusively as possible. It was a rather silent ride (at least on their part) back to Coronado—Beautiful, though driving south along the moonlit shoreline, and Annie and I regretted our little strike not at all.

I did have one other incipient romance early in this period. It turned out tragically, but, I guess served as a purpose in that it enabled me to formulate a philosophy that helped me through the troubled and sometimes terrifying times of the decade that was to follow.

I can't remember how we met—probably at some event at the wine mess, but we seemed to be mutually attracted—a six foot tall redheaded Marine pilot and I. Having learned my lessons from my previous experience I saw to it that we were moving very slowly—dating only two or three times a week but finding we had so many common interests. I was really beginning to look forward to our times together.

I picked up the newspaper one morning to read on the ferry on my way to school in San Diego, and on the front page was a picture of a Marine fighter plane that had crashed up at Torrey Pines late on the previous day. The pilot had been my newly found friend, and he had been killed. As an extra added attraction to the picture the newspaper had placed an arrow pointing to one of his boots which had been torn off by the force of the crash and which was lying near the tangled wreckage of the plane.

It was my first personal brush with death by air, and for a

couple of days I was really unable to cope with it. Tom finally came to my rescue. He sat me down and gave me a lecture which I have remembered every since.

During the late 30's there were extant some seven (eight if you counted the Langley which was really a sea-plane tender) aircraft carriers, and therefore the number of Navy pilots was not that large and like an overgrown fraternity. Everyone knew or knew of everyone else, and not a week went by without some friend or acquaintance becoming a victim of his profession. As Tom said, if I was going to go to pieces every time this happened I would never survive in this milieu of which I loved so much being a part. He was right, and I took his advice, and though not easily and not all at once, I finally acquired the ability to accept these sudden cessations of life—not without compassion but also with dispassion—as something seen through the wrong end of a telescope from which I was totally disassociated. It sounds cruel, but it was the only way to survive.

I had planned on staying for about three weeks, but it turned out to be such heaven for a young, single female that I stayed on. We all had a simply marvelous time. There were only about forty young unattached females in Coronado, with some 250 aviation cadets, not to mention bachelor officers in the regular Navy, so we had no lack of invitations out. In fact we became rather choosy, and of an evening used to turn down telephone invitations until someone we wanted to go out with would call.

This was near the end of the depression, and though I really looked, jobs weren't all that easy to come by. That's why I went to business school in San Diego, where I met Betty Potter who lived on Point Loma. We were most compatible—even had mutual friends back east—and we became close friends.

After ten months at San Diego College of Commerce, during which time I learned more practical English than I had in four years at Smith I decided to go out and get a job. They were hiring stenographers at the State Relief Bureau so I applied, but when they saw I had a degree from Smith and had taken a course in sociology (required to graduate) they said I'd do better as a social worker than as a stenographer; the pay was $10 more a month. So a social worker I became, subsequently learning to my chagrin that whereas I had six years of French, four of Latin and one of German, most of my case load spoke Spanish or Italian. So much for college cumulative learning! I earned the magnificent sum of $100 a month, which was adequate to live on in the late '30's.

I lived with Wo and Tom in their small house at 736 I Avenue for some eighteen months. Even though there were only about two bedrooms so that I shared one with their small son, Mark, I found the living most pleasant and with the self-centeredness of youth never stopped to think that they might

13

I and Betty Harris, on our penthouse roof.

Rest and Relaxation inside the penthouse.

possibly be happier without me. They never so said but put up cheerfully with my comings and goings at odd hours, myriad phone calls and alternate moods of elation and depression which were in direct proportion to the fullness of my social calendar.

One Saturday night, I was between beaus and therefore dateless and extremely bored. Tom had been over in the valley dove hunting all day and had come home with quite a bag of the poor little things. I must have been extremely callous at the time to have been able to do it (couldn't possibly today), but I was helping him pluck them. We were drinking beer as we worked and by the time we had all the little bodies laid out (around eleven p.m.) we were feeling no pain. Wo had long since given up on us and gone to bed. We decided Coronado was being a very dull town for a Saturday night and that we should do something about it—so we went out on the back steps. I screamed as loudly as I could, and Tom shot off the gun he had been hunting with that day. Then we sat down on the pack porch to see what would happen, which was exactly nothing—no reaction at all. We might as well have been out in the middle of Death Valley. In disgust we retired for the night. None of the neighbors mentioned hearing noises in the night, and we, feeling rather foolish never did either. So much for rebellion against the local mores.

In February of 1939 the fleet took off for eight weeks of war games in the Pacific. Tom and Wo gave up their house, and she went back east to show off Mark to various relatives, I took a room in an old Victorian house on C Avenue. When I walked by this house during my last Coronado visit I noticed a sign designating it as a historic land mark. Not because of my three months sojourn I'm afraid. I paid fifteen dollars a month for a lovely room about half the size of Grand Central Station, my own bath and even a little balcony.

A few houses down the street lived Lollie McCormick. Her husband was also at sea leaving her with their two children who were only a year apart. Mac believed in the old Navy adage regarding wives—always leave them barefoot and pregnant. A friend was visiting her, Betty Harris who was just getting over an unfortunate marriage. I took my meals with them, and since I had no phone of my own gave their number as mine to prospective dates. Between Betty and me Lollie was soon taking messages and making dates for us to the extent that we started calling her Madam McCormick, and she reciprocated by calling us her girls.

In the spring of 1939 Betty and I took a penthouse together. It was so-called because it was on the roof of a 3-story apartment building, The Vanderbilt, but it was really just an over-sized game room made mostly of beaver board, divided by such into living room, dining room, and bedroom. We had the whole roof, though, and since Coronado had very few tall buildings at that time, we had a beautiful view of the town, the ocean, the bay, and the strand. The rent was $30 a month.

Betty Potter used to stay with us quite frequently. One Saturday afternoon after a game of tennis, she and I were enjoying strawberry sundaes at the Coronado Drug Store when up came Al Masters, a pilot in Scouting 2 (attached to the Lexington), who stopped to chat. I introduced him to Betty, and thus began a whirlwind courtship which resulted in plans for a wedding on May 5, 1939. I was to be maid of honor and Bob (whom I still hadn't met) was to be best man. It seems he and Al had been bunk mates and best friends all through flight training in Pensacola, but then Al had been ordered to San Diego to Scouting Two on the Lexington and Bob to Fighting Five on the Yorktown. The latter had been stationed in Norfolk, but was coming to San Diego for its new home port that spring. It got held up coming through the Panama Canal, didn't get to San Diego until a week or so after the wedding, so they had to get another friend, Ed Stebbins, to fill in as best man. He was the one with whom I had the ersatz romance when I first came to Coronado, and I don't know whether he was afraid he would or I would succumb to the excitement of the hour, but at the end of the wedding ceremony after I had handed Betty back her bouquet and straightened her train I turned to take his arm to find he had fled precipitously and left me to descend the alter and walk back down the aisle alone. I was annoyed at first, but actually it turned out to be rather a heady feeling—smiling and nodding at the congregation as I paraded by in solitary splendor—Betty and Al having run down the aisle and long since disappeared.

So, once again, Bob and I didn't meet. In fact we had been chasing each other all over the country, and when we finally met, it was just a dull thud, no bells ringing, no starry eyes. When I was at Smith, from 1932 to 1936, Bob spent two years, 1934-1936, at nearby Springfield College. At Smith I lived at Hubbard House, where Bob would come on occasion to take out a Springfield girl, but we never met there. One of my Smith friends Em Jones Neff lived on Maple Street in Springfield and I spent many weekends with her, but we didn't meet there. The summer after I graduated I spent with Wo and Tom, who was going through flight training in Pensacola. Bob turned up there for flight training, but again we didn't meet.

That isn't to say I didn't have an interesting summer because I didn't meet him there. There were lots of bachelor officers, and while everyone went to bed at ten o'clock week nights so they would be bright-eyed and bushy-tailed for flight training in the morning, on weekends they made up for it even though there were only about two places in which to whoop it up—The

16

Officers' Club on the Air Station and the Barn, a private club in town.

Pensacola, itself, was really a one horse town fifty years ago, or perhaps it should have been called a cow town. The officers all lived in small rented cottages scattered near the road between the town and the Air Station. There must have been farms there, too, as there were plenty of cows around, and they had open range—could wander whenever their bovine hearts desired. It was the exception rather than the rule if one was not awakened sometime in the night by the crunch-munching of a herd of cows dining happily on the lawn under the bedroom window. They were also somewhat of a highway hazard. White or yellow lines meant nothing to them, and they wandered happily up and down the roads. They were quite frequently hit by a car driven by a hurrying late night returner from the town to the Base. The cow always seemed to walk away, though. It was the car that was left mortally wounded in the middle of the road.

What I remember most about Pensacola, though, was the temperature and the humidity. Both were so high that clothes mildewed just hanging in the closet. Both were so intense that getting my hair done always became a Catch 22 situation. It was wet, of course, from the shampoo and wave lotion then used, but when the hot air from the dryer hit my scalp it caused rivulets of perspiration which kept my hair from ever dying. It was so everlasting that Wo and I drank iced tea all day and continually crunched the ice that was in it. In the thirties air conditioning in private homes was unheard of. We found this very cooling, though when Tom was home the sound drove him up the wall—particularly at the dinner table where, due to his prodigious appetite and slow eating habits, we had to sit for upwards of a half an hour waiting for him to finish (crunching away to make the time pass). Finally Tom took to setting his sword on the table beside him and warning us that one more crunch and we were in for it—nothing as gory as being skewered but being rapped smartly across the knuckles with the flat of it. It surely spoiled our pleasure, but it probably saved our teeth, and Tom really did have to have some means of keeping his mini-harem in line. In spite of the above vicissitudes it was a delightful summer.

When Bob and I finally made contact, it was at the home of our mutual friends, Al and Betty Masters. After they got back from their honeymoon they lived for a while in her family's house on Point Loma, and as the weather got warmer I got into the habit of going there for a swim two or three times a week after work. Every time I went Bob seemed to be there too, and since he had no car at the time I'd end up driving him back to Coronado. Since I was then 'going steady' (in the then current phrase) with an ensign who had just been transferred to Norfolk, I wasn't interested in any other male companionship so I just tolerated his presence. Things drifted along with me being faithful to my absent beau, and Bob hanging around on the periphery of my life.

One Saturday night when I was alone in the penthouse I heard a loud pounding at the door, and there I found one Robin Lindsay, a friend of Betty's, who had obviously been drinking. I couldn't get him to go away, so I finally offered to help him look for Betty. We set out in his car, and it soon became evident he was just looking for an out-of-the-way place to park. I asked him to stop so I could get some cigarettes (standard protection against unwanted advances) at the Rose Bowl, the town's most popular bar. There I found Bob sitting at the bar, celebrating his 26th birthday all by himself. I sat down to tell him what was going on with Robin and asked if he'd take me home, which he did. When we came out of the bar Robin's car was gone but I thought nothing of it.

I was rather embarrassed at having to ask Bob to drive me home, so I told him just to let me out and not bother walking me up the four flights to the penthouse. Once inside I turned on the lights, went to the bedroom, and there found Robin asleep on the bed. (I learned later that he was known for climbing into any old bed after imbibing too much and once boarded the wrong carrier and passed out in the wrong bunk.)

I was so furious that I filled a large pitcher with cold water; went to the bedroom and shook him, promising that if he didn't remove himself from the premises immediately I'd dump it on him. Much to my surprise he got up and staggered out of the house and down the stairs. I locked all the doors and windows and went to bed.

As it happened this incident served a good purpose, as Bob and I drifted into a very comfortable relationship. By then he had his own car, (the one which later gave us such an eventful trip across country), and we began to go out together frequently. We went to softball games around town (free); or to the zoo (10 cents); or wandered around Balboa Park (also free). I was really a cheap date, but we found ourselves growing fonder and fonder of each other. Finally Bob started asking me to marry him every time we went out. I kept putting him off because I was still supposed to be waiting for my beau on the east coast. But as my children remember, once their father decided he wanted something he didn't give up until he got it.

Soon I decided the only thing to do was to get away for a while so I could get a perspective on things. So I took my two weeks' vacation and all my savings to fly to Washington to visit my father, who was then living there with my aunt.

It was the first time I had ever flown, and I was not without a few butterflies at the thought. However, Fighting Five was having a cocktail party that afternoon at the wine mess, and as my plane didn't leave until eight p.m. I packed my suitcase, put it in Bob's car, and off we went to join the festivities. I think Bob realized my trepidation because he kept replacing my half empty glass with a full one until I was wandering around in an alcohol induced state of euphoria. For a while I could probably have flown without the plane.

Bob had wanted to tell everyone at the party that we were thinking of getting married on my return. I wasn't all that sure in my own mind, and thought it would hurt him less if we waited until I came back in case I didn't. However, much to my chagrin he did tell the skipper after swearing him to secrecy.

We left the party in plenty of time for Bob to drive me to the airport in San Diego, board the plane with me, strap me into my seat, threaten the stewardess with murder and mayhem if she didn't make my welfare her first priority and leave.

It was a pleasant, painless maiden flight—probably because I didn't remember much of it. I had to change airports in L.A., and the stewardess kept her word to Bob and saw me aboard the bus to the second airport. I do remember climbing into the strange little berth—more like a hammock than a regular bunk—and sleeping peacefully until I was awakened the next morning in time to wrestle myself into my clothes before landing in D.C. surprisingly bright-eyed and bushy-tailed in spite of my somewhat rowdy launching party the night before.

Two days after I got to Washington I received the following letter from Bob.

VF5 F.A.D.
San Diego, California
Sept. 16

My darling!
This is the first day in many that we haven't been together, and I miss you more than anything in the world.

There are so many things I wanted to say as you left, and I wanted to be alone with you, but everything was so rushed.

Please forgive me for being so inconsiderate, but, Anne honey I was so excited I couldn't think of anything but your going away from me for such a long time.

Gosh how I miss you and want you to come back to me for always. I must get out of the week's cruise somehow I have so many things to do before you get back (He didn't, but he managed to survive).

Darling, I love you and for two weeks am going to be very unhappy. Have a grand visit and get anything you want—we'll worry about it later together.

Hope your Father and Aunt will approve of me.
All my love,

19

Bob

# # #

I was to receive 5 more of the same ilk the two weeks I was in Washington and in the next six years some two hundred and fifty more (all answered by me in kind)—a bond between us during those tumultuous times. I have all of Bob's stored away and was never able to reread them until recently after going to a 45th reunion of VFN-90 where we all shared a marvelously nostalgic three days. I could read them not only without sadness but with a feeling of going back in time and living once more all those times together. I have therefore included some of them where pertinent and where I feel it enhances those years of our lives. On my return trip it took eighteen hours from D.C. back to L.A. on a sleeper plane.

On the way in to L.A. on the plane, the pilot called me up to the cockpit. Bob was on the two-way radio from the tower. Hearing his voice was all I needed to realize once and for all that he was the one I wanted to be with for the rest of my life—or, as it turned out, the rest of his life. So when he asked me on the air if I had made up my mind, I couldn't say "Yes!" fast enough. Nothing like a proposal for all the world to hear.

We spent the trip from Los Angeles to Coronado making plans. It was common knowledge that either the Yorktown or the Enterprise (they were sister ships) was being transferred to Pearl Harbor in two weeks, so, as we didn't want to wait for heaven knew how long, we thought we'd better get married the following Friday so there wasn't sufficient time (or money) for an engagement ring. In fact I didn't have a diamond solitaire until our second wedding anniversary. It was a lovely one, but nothing could ever outshine my little diamond encircled wedding band with which he me wed at 4:30 p.m. on Friday afternoon October 6, 1939. Instead I wore all that week before our wedding Bob's Naval Aviator's ring brought down to size by about a half roll of adhesive tape. I wear it again now on my right hand—permanently cut down to my size. Bob engaged the church and the minister the very next day. He was the first cadet in Fighting Five to get married, but shortly, what with bad news in Europe and the fleet being moved around, it got to be very difficult to find a time when the church and minister were available. Before long there was a series of sort of assembly line weddings. I telegraphed my father and aunt and the latter came out, but my poor father had just had a stroke and was unable to come. Bob said his parents couldn't make it, so I gave it no further thought.

I had to be at work the Monday after I got back and Bob had a lot more free time, so he made all the wedding plans.

20

Unfortunately, when I got home from work on Tuesday I found he was in the dispensary with a sore throat. It was lucky he'd made the arrangements and found a little duplex, because he stayed in sick bay until Friday noon, October 6, and we were to be married at 4:30. Around 10 o'clock that morning the doctor came in with a horse-sized syringe and said he had a new drug that would kill or cure. Bob decided to give it a try and took the shot. For about an hour he thought he was going to die, then suddenly he felt marvelous. He found out later it was penicillin, which was still in the experimental stage and released only to the services. Luckily, it really did the trick.

It was such a hectic week that my recollections of our wedding are hazy in certain aspects, but other incidents are crystal clear.

I remember having my hair done the day before and for some unknown reason having it parted in the middle for the first time—and thereafter being so superstitious that I would never let the part be changed in all our married life.

I remember that on the morning of our wedding I realized I had no wedding hat to go with the lovely teal blue afternoon dress I had bought from the shop where Betty worked. So she and I hurried over to San Diego—me with my hair bound up in a kerchief because it was damp and misting, wearing an old red wool dress with no hem and old white huaraches so stretched out they flopped every time I took a step. Some beautiful bride! Did find a hat, tho'.

I remember that about 3:30 Betty Masters called frantically to say Al had radioed from his plane somewhere near the Coronados Islands to say he was flying as fast as possible but didn't know whether he'd make it or not in time to be our best man. He arrived at the church a few minutes late and a little dissheveled from changing from flight gear to dress blues in the car while Betty drove.

I remember standing alone in the middle of the church aisle for what seemed like hours while Tom (who gave me away) went back to the vestibule because he had forgotten to hang up his uniform cap there. I've always wondered if he did it on purpose.

I remember at the reception trying to shoot champagne corks through the ventilator in the ceiling of Wo's kitchen.

I remember Al's sneaking us away from the reception and taking us to our little duplex so Bob could change from his uniform to his civvies. While he was changing, up the stairs came my aunt. She disapproved highly of drinking so just took a glass of champagne to toast the bride and groom, but Tom kept filling up her glass and proposing toasts and soon she as as happily pixillated as everyone else and insisted on Tom's driving her over in his old jalopy of a truck to see the apartment while we were still in it. We slipped down the stairs to the garage where we

21

Honeymoon at Warner's Hot Springs. October 6-8, 1939.

thought we had successfully hidden the car, but someone had found it, disconnected a couple of the spark plugs and tied tin cans and a "Just Married" sign to the rear bumper. We clattered and lurched down Orange Avenue and arrived at the ferry slip just in time to catch the ferry and leave our pursuers on the edge of the ferry slip. Fortunately Bob had no trouble reconnecting the spark plugs and disentangling the tin cans on our ten minute ride across the bay to San Diego.

I remember half way up to Warner's Hot Springs in the lowering, misty evening suddenly getting cold feet and telling Bob I had changed my mind and wanted to go home. Luckily, he had no trouble talking me out of that silly idea.

I remember the next morning how two Indian squaws giggled and chattered between themselves when they came in to clean. We were sitting decorously but blissfully by the fire in our bathrobes, but only one twin bed had been slept in, and there was rice all over the floor. It took me months to figure out how the rice had gotten into my suitcase. I had given it to Wo for safekeeping never dreaming she'd fink on her own sister.

We had a small but perfect wedding in the Episcopal Church in Coronado, with only about eight of my closest friends so my side of the church was relatively empty. Bob invited everyone he saw all week so his side was really jammed. My sister and Tom gave us a very nice reception at their house, champagne and cake cut with Bob's sword, rice as we left and all the things that are fun at weddings.

We had a wonderful two-day honeymoon at Warner's Hot Springs. When we first got there Bob sent a telegram to his family telling them we were married, and I was surprised he hadn't done this earlier. It seems he was afraid they'd rush out and try to change his mind, as they had done previously with his older brother Russ, when he was at the University of Pennsylvania. Russ and Sis were engaged for about ten years before they were married; quite a contrast to our brief romantic period—three weeks of courtship and a five day engagement.

Thanks to my job we had only a weekend honeymoon. Bob could have gotten leave, but I'd used all my vacation time, and we had decided I'd keep on working to augment Bob's magnificent salary of $200 a month. So back to work we both went on Monday morning.

Before we were married I didn't know much about Bob's career in the Navy. I knew he went to Springfield College, but left in 1937 to enlist in the new Aviation Cadet program at Squantum Naval Training Station. From there he went to Pensacola for his actual flight training. And when he received his wings he became an Aviation Cadet. The Cadets were a new breed which the proper Naval Academy Navy had no precedent for, and didn't know how to classify. They were neither fish,

Bob in his carefree bachelor days in Norfolk in 1937.

flesh, nor fowl; they all attended college but were not products of Annapolis. They were above the ratings of enlisted men but below the ranks of officers. They wore a single stripe on their sleeves, about an eighth of an inch narrower than that of an ensign. The main difficulty was in the social pecking order; since they were officially neither officers nor enlisted men they were welcome in neither stratum.

I first heard of Aviation Cadets when I was visiting my sister and brother-in-law in Pensacola, where Tom was going through flight training. I think they were admitted to the Officers' Club but not to the private, exclusive Navy clubs. They were spoken of quite disdainfully, like the family black sheep, and I was told tactfully that one didn't associate with them—I don't think I even saw one while I was there.

By the time I got to Coronado the following summer, though, things were beginning to change. There were so many cadets by this time that they made up a large percentage of the pilots. Furthermore, they were proving to be every bit as proficient in the cockpit of an airplane, or in the confines of a cocktail party as their Naval Academy confreres, so they began to be accepted. Finally in 1939 President Roosevelt proclaimed the Aviation Cadets officers and gentlemen. They received commissions as ensigns and were allowed to marry after two years in the service, just in time for Bob and me. Their pay was increased from $150 a month to $200 a month, plenty to live on when you consider that rent was $50 a month, and the grocery bill seldom exceeded $20.

Actually, though they weren't supposed to marry before their two years were up, quite a few had done so. They kept their wives sub rosa in a rather seedy apartment in Coronado known to us all as the Pink Palace because it was built of pink stucco, what else? They were happy when they no longer had to sneak around corners pretending that their wives were just good friends or passing fancies.

Cadets were not barred from the Officers' Club on the Air Station but they weren't made to feel comfortable there, which bothered them not at all. They had their own wine mess located right next to their quarters—nice little bungalows, relics of the time when North Island was inhabited by the Army. The wine mess was a lovely big building with a huge patio, several large living rooms, and bar presided over by a Filipino mess boy, Vic, who knew everybody and could call us by name and knew what we like to drink. Can you imagine—bourbon was 12 cents a drink, scotch 15 cents, and a not bad bottle of champagne just 75 cents? Cigarettes were 8 cents a pack. Drinking wasn't one of the things I'd learned at Smith, and as I reached the drinking age just at the end of prohibition I didn't know much about it. I always ordered scotch and soda because that was what the

25

sophisticates ordered in the movies, but loathed the taste and drank it because it was the thing to do. Luckily Bob switched me over to bourbon soon after we met, and it was always our drink, not even with branch water but just on the rocks.

Chapter 3

The cadets also had a marvelous swimming pool, much more elegant than the one at the Officers' Club. We lucky females and our dates spent Saturdays and Sundays during the dry season artistically draped on the sand in the first of the lastex bathing suits, sipping drinks, eating hamburgers, and engaging in cheerful bandinage. On one such Saturday a little yellow Piper Cub flew noisily overhead, causing us all to look up. When we lowered our eyes it was a strange sight—not a male in the beach area, just a bunch of open-mouthed females, half eaten hamburgers, and half empty glasses stuck in the sand. The boys had recognized the sound of a plane in trouble and were across the bridge and at the edge of the golf course (now filled in and covered with private homes, in one of which Betty Ferguson lives) almost before the plane crash-landed on the fifth green. No great harm done—just a facial cut for the pilot, an aviation cadet reputed to be very religious. He was taking his girl for a ride in a rented plane, and the boys said as they filtered back to their warm drinks, cool girls and cold hamburgers, that if he had kept his hands on the stick instead of folding them to pray, he wouldn't have crashed.

Incidentally, that pool is no longer there. Betty Ferguson and I went looking for it when I was in Coronado last summer, and though the wine mess building still remains, the rest is all lawn and shrubbery. There should be a plaque to the good times we had there. Sic transit gloria mundi!

Bob got an early start with the Aviation Cadets. From Pensacola he was ordered to Fighting Squadron Five which was attached to the Yorktown, based in Norfolk, V. It's probably a good thing I didn't know too much about his bachelor days around Norfolk and in the Caribbean. He was part of a foursome, all cadets, all single, all fighter pilots: Tommy McKnight, Mike Leonard, and Mario Guerrieri, and I guess they saw everything there was to see and did everything there was to do. But in the spring of 1939 the Yorktown was ordered to San Diego to be based there, and at long last we met, overcame a few hurdles already described and were married. We settled down to a period of domestic bliss in the little duplex Bob had rented. After about three weeks I gave up my job with no regrets; I was such a neophyte at housework that the laundry piled up in the bathroom and the dust in all the corners. And Bob refused to have anything to do with housework in any way, shape or form. He didn't have to be at North Island until 9 a.m. and was through by 4 p.m., while I had to be in San Diego by 8 a.m. and didn't get out until 5 p.m. I had to work Saturday morning, and he didn't and we hated to waste what time we had on something so mundane as housework. We spent an idyllic five months,

The happy B. and G. outside their first home in Coronado
—October 1939.

marred by only some minor incidents.

In January I met the first members of Bob's family, an uncle and cousin from Wheatland, Wyoming, who were on a business trip to San Diego. We invited them for dinner, and I was going to show them what a marvel of domesticity Bob had married. The whole thing was a disaster. I had steak, which to me was very special, but they owned a cattle ranch and had it twice a day. I misread the directions and rolled the biscuits too thin; they looked and tasted like large-sized poker chips. For dessert I'd made a lemon pie, using two lemons from a neighboring tree which were the size of small grapefruit. The receipt said the juice of two lemons, and I'm so literal minded I used the juice of both lemons and the resultant filling was runny and puckered your mouth. We had ice cream for dessert.

We had our first fight on the golf course about three weeks after we were married. I had a bad habit of hitting my drive off the tee so that it often flew at right angles over the fence and out of bounds. Previously someone had always rushed over to hold up the fence for me to climb through. So on this afternoon when I did the usual, I went and stood patiently by the fence. Much to my indignation Bob just kept walking straight down the fairway to where his ball lay right in the middle. When I asked him if he wasn't going to hold up the fence, he just laughed and told me to do it myself. It was too far out of the way. We didn't speak for the rest of the nine holes, that is, I didn't—he thought it hilarious.

We had our second fight about a week later, and it, too had to do with golf though a cheese souffle was the real catalyst. Tom and Bob decided to play golf at Rancho Santa Fe on their Wednesday afternoon off. I was surprised and somewhat miffed that Bob would want to do anything without me on his time off (remember, I was a bride of only a month) so I wasn't too pleasant to him before he left. I don't think he even noticed it, but I felt remorseful after he had gone and decided to make amends by having a very special dinner for him when he got home.

As I said, I was such a new bride I hadn't yet learned to expect a husband (at least, mine) home at any given time after a session on the golf course and an ensuing visit to the clubhouse bar was really ridiculous. I happily constructed a cheese souffle and put it in the oven so it would be ready precisely at 6 p.m.—the time Bob had said he would be home. At 6 it was as beautiful, golden brown cumulus cloud-like construction. At 6:30 it had deflated somewhat and was a dark chocolate brown color as I was trying to keep it warm in the oven, and it was becoming slightly overdone. At seven when Bob walked jocularly in the door, it was flatter than the well-known pancake, black, and looked very similar to the prune whip I had made for Tom a couple of years before. Bob was served it for dinner, anyway, along with a large helping of lugubrious silence which lasted for another hour or two until I finally realized how ridiculous I was being. I never could stand being mad at Bob for long. He promised to let me know when he was going to be that late again, and I promised not to start dinner until he did. Happily (thought I feared otherwise when Bob left me for my brother-in-law that afternoon) the honeymoon was not yet over.

The prewar Navy had an intriguing system for formal calls. It was discontinued during World War II, and I keep forgetting to ask if it was resumed afterwards though I rather doubt it since everything became so much more informal as time went by. I wonder how many Navy personnel are still around who remember boat cloaks, railroad pants, swabs and fore and aft hats.

I digress. As to the calling. It was really a kind of game to see who could outwit whom. The rules at best as I can remember were that when a new couple came to the squadron, they called on the Skipper and his wife, but all the other married officers and wives had first to call on the new couple who then had to return each call. The hours were from four until six; the costume quite formal—afternoon wear—for the wives, hats with veils and white gloves and for the husbands their most elegant civilian suits. Calling cards were a must. He left two because he was calling on both man and wife, but she left one because she was only calling on the wife.

The fun part was either timing your call when no one was home and you could leave your cards and therefore get credit for having been there or else seeing how embarrassing a situation you could catch the callees in by calling unexpectedly. Unfortunately, we once got hoist on our own petard. We had just gotten in from playing tennis. I was glowing, to say the least, and had torn the shoulder of my tennis dress frustratingly trying to smash a forehand by Bob who always beat me at tennis, too. Tom's Dad had given us a wild duck he had shot on a recent hunting trip, and I was in the kitchen with my hands covered with flour trying to figure how in the dickens you cook a duck when the doorbell rang. It was the Skipper and his wife (what ensign of two months and his wife weren't in awe of a Lt. Cdr.?) returning our call.

Whenever the squadrons went aboard the carriers for maneuvers, time would crawl slowly, but how lovely it was on a Friday to hear the sound of a whole air group flying ashore. When the noise got loud enough, each wife dashed out to the air station as if she hadn't seen her husband for months. Otherwise time flew by happily until suddenly it was the first of April.

Bob had his tonsils out and hemorrhaged so had to stay in the hospitals for two weeks. It seemed an interminable time to us, but much worse was to come. In April Bob went off with the fleet for six weeks of war games, and I sadly left our honeymoon cottage to move back in with my sister who was expecting her second child momentarily. Also there were her 3 year-old son Mark, her maid and good friend to us all, Mattie Mae, and my friend Betty Masters, who was luckier than most of us. Her husband Al had been transferred to Hawaii and she would soon be on her way via the Matson Line to join him there.

# # #

Honolulu off starboard bow
April 25, 1940

Anne my darling,
If I could tell you what's in my heart—I love you more than I'll ever be able to say. How I wish you were in Honolulu tonight and I would be seeing you tomorrow.

We're just passing through the Harbor and have just finished a beautiful searchlight parade of all the fleet. It was a marvelous sight and must have meant a great deal to those ashore waiting for their husbands. There are well over 100 vessels and each had several lights going—all in set patterns and moving in order. It was very well done and lighted up the sea like day.

About our trip—it had a few interesting side lines.

First, when we sailed from Lahaina (sp?) for battle, we launched and flew over all the islands. It was really beautiful, and we saw everything so plainly. We flew over a big volcano on Maui about 1000' high and down into the crater for a ways. The crater was seven miles around and about 5000' high going straight down to the sea, and all along at points were beautiful waterfalls dropping clear to the sea. The water was a clear blue color, and there were many beautiful beaches. Islands are quite colorful and very mountainous.

As we sailed past the island of Hawaii we could see the live volcano, Mauna Loa, erupting. Very pretty with fingers of flame shooting up.

We didn't fly until Saturday, but Sun., Mond., and Tues. we took off each day at 0500 and kept going pretty much all day. Had a couple of scraps with the Lexington, but they bombed the Yorktown, and we were out of the last part of the problem and put into Lahaina before the others. Everything went ok and got along fine but tired.

We started the problem on Monday, April 15 and sailed south to 4 degrees—darn near the equator and sure wished we could have crossed and taken initiation to shell backs.

I wish you could have been with me Tues, morning. We took off at 0430 with a full moon and it was marvelous—so beautiful I can't describe it. There were just hundreds of clouds that reflected all shades of colors. Later the biggest, brightest sunrise I ever saw just put the poor old moon in the back seat, and the whole sky just blossomed out like a beautiful garden. How anyone seeing that view could think of fighting is beyond me.

Take good care of yourself for me, sweetie. I'd die if anything happened to you.

I'm feeling grand and in good shape. Still have a big tummy, but it's much harder. Play badminton every day.

> *I love you darling,*
> *Bob xxxxxxxx*

#

Bob became a shellback finally when he was attached to the Belleau Wood just after she was involved in the Baker and Tarawa raids September 1 to September 18, 1943. His diploma hangs on the den wall. The actual date and longitude are censored due to wartime regulations.

This was the only tour of sea duty during which Bob could give times, and descriptions. Shortly censorship was put into effect, and anything that could give any sort of clue to any sort of enemy fell under the censor's scissors.

> *Honolulu*
> *April 26*

My dearest Anne,

Gee, honey, I'm lonesome. I miss you so and I want to come home.

Going to write a letter each day. I won't have much to say, but at least I can be happy while writing to you.

We docked this morning, and so far I haven't seen or heard a great deal as I have the duty and stayed aboard. We are at Pearl Harbor Navy Yard and some twenty miles from the city.

I'm wondering how to get in touch with Betty and Al. Will look up Tommy Blackburn, too.

Tommy McKnight caught the first boat shore and by now probably doesn't know his own name. I guess in his own way he's having fun, but, darling, I'm happier than anyone just writing to you and seeing your picture.

Every night I cross out a day on the calendar, and how slowly the days pass. We've passed the middle, though, darling, and before you know it you'll be awakened by the noise of our planes coming back to land

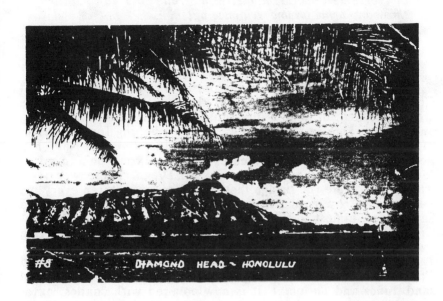

DIAMOND HEAD - HONOLULU

POST CARD

CORRESPONDENCE   ADDRESS ONLY

Mrs. R.V. McCullough
959 E Ave
Coronado
California

at North Island. Meet me, won't you? so I can run and
throw my arms around you once again.
                        Your loving husband,

# # #

We all envied Betty, for the departure of the fleet had left
Coronado a manless town filled with lonely, frustrated females.
We had settled down to a dull routine of golf, tennis, swimming
and some bridge in the evenings. We kept hoping for the arrival
of Wo's baby to break the monotony. At that time the Navy had
no facilities for maternity cases, and everyone had to go to
Mercy Hospital across the bay in San Diego. There were two
ways to get there (no bridge then); by ferry, which ran every ten
minutes until 2 a.m. and took about ten minutes, or by driving to
San Ysidro, almost to the Mexican border, then over to National
City and into San Diego, which meant seventeen miles of driving
over sand dunes, lonely even in the middle of the day.

This route was over the Silver Strand that connected
Coronado to the mainland and consisted of the aforementioned
sand dunes and ice plant. It is now covered with condos, naval
quarters and quays on the bay side, but in the late thirties it was
a deserted mecca for those wishing to park for a little privacy
and dalliance. There was only one problem. If the car stayed
parked too long in one spot the wheels settled into the sand and
wouldn't move when discretion said it was time to go. The
occupants then had to plod through the soft sand, shamefacedly
to seek help from a passing motorist or else had to walk all the
way to the Clock a small bar of dubious distinction at the end of
the Strand, where the patrons stared at them with knowing leers.

On the evening of April 12 we sat around talking, Wo
suddenly went to get her suitcase. She said there was no hurry,
but I was all for going over and waiting outside the hospital. Wo
refused to budge until the pains quickened and finally the water
broke just as we heard the 2 a.m. ferry whistle. There was
nothing to do but start trekking by car over the dunes, probably
the most nerve-wracking trip I ever took. At one point the
rubber top to the foot brake pedal fell off, but Wo said
frantically there was no time to stop, so on we went through the
night with her pains getting closer and with me gritting my
teeth, and groping for the metal spike that was the brake. We
drove through the worst sections of San Diego but at that hour
there was no traffic or strange characters hanging around. As we
neared the hospital I hit a large traffic turtle in the middle of a
curve. We seemed to go ten feet in the air, coming down with
such a thud I thought it would precipitate the baby into the cold,
cruel world. But we made it to the hospital, and twenty minutes
after our arrival I had a new niece, Pattie. I spent the rest of the

night dozing in a chair in Wo's room and took the 7 o'clock ferry back to Coronado. Then I went for a golf lesson, playing the best game I've ever played before or since. The pro said I was so tired I was completely relaxed.

The baby created a diversion, but then things went along routinely for a while. I drove Betty to L.A. and put her on the Matsonia for Hawaii and Al, envying her all the way. Came back to Coronado and with other lonely wives resumed the daily athletic routine. We all counted the days till the war games would be over and Coronado would again become a normal Navy town, with all our husbands home.

One morning we awakened to find the town in pandemonium and the media in seventh heaven; the Pacific fleet had suddenly disappeared. It was rumored to be heading back to the states; it was rumored to be heading for Australia, or for the Panama Canal and thence to Europe. We were like panic-stricken sheep, running around trying to believe the good rumors and ignore the bad ones. The fleet showed up at Pearl Harbor about a week later, then to every navy wife's consternation it was learned that it would be based in Hawaii and wouldn't come back to San Diego in the foreseeable future. There was a concerted rush by every female with a husband in the fleet to book passage on one of the three means of transportation. The Matson Steamship line was the most popular way to go, and its two ships were booked solid for 3 months. Or one could fly on the Yankee Clipper, which I think flew only once a week. Then there was a Japanese steamship line which nobody trusted, but we'd have walked to get there. I was on all three waiting lists.

Then the fleet disappeared again and everybody canceled. I could have gotten passage on anything, but was afraid to go because the same rumors persisted. We'd get our hopes up, then everything would go down the drain again. So we reluctantly went back to our old routine, listening in vain for good news on the 15-minute radio program "Navy News". This came on at 5:45 every night, and professed to have the inside track on the fleet's movements, but actually knew less about it than we did.

# # #

Honolulu
7 May
Cheer up, Anne my darling,
We just have to be good sailors and hold tight until we really know what's going to happen. I hope it's nothing more serious than the renewal of a rather bad fleet problem and that we will be but a week or so late getting back.
Here everything so far is all mixed and mostly

35

rumors, and I'll let you know anything just as soon as I know it is definitely true. Any important news or rumors you may hear be careful of, and if anything so every important happens I'll wire you, honey.

Thank God we had those perfect five months together. Nothing can take them away from us.

> *Your loving husband*
> *Bob*

Honolulu
8 May

Anne, my darling,

I am just about at the end of my hopes.

The radio just broadcasted the news that the fleet is staying in Honolulu an undetermined length of time for another war games.

You will hear about I'm sure and probably already have by radio and newspaper.

Honolulu
8 May

My darling,

How the days drag. Rumors, rumors, rumors all day and all night, and nobody knows a darn thing. Everyone is so bitter, no smiles, no laughs, and things don't seem to matter. Everyone just wants to get home.

We fly in the morning, and I think it will help everyone. I hope so. We take off about 0900, land on one of the islands, operate from land all day and return to the ship in late afternoon. Tomorrow is our first try and should be interesting. We are scheduled to do the same thing Thurs. and Fri. and then go in and have liberty over the weekend.

Next week we still don't have any dope about.

Keep the old chin up, darling, and soon your salty old husband will be back to you. Thought of you keeps me going through these uncertain days.

Bremerton
25 May

My darling. After my call to you tonight I ran out on the gang so I could have the room to myself to write to you. I can't stand this much longer. When I think of you and me so far apart and now knowing when it will end.

You must know how badly I wanted to have you here, my darling, but please forgive me when I thought it best for you to stay away. It is so far and so uncertain. Have tried all ways of getting leave, and there just isn't any

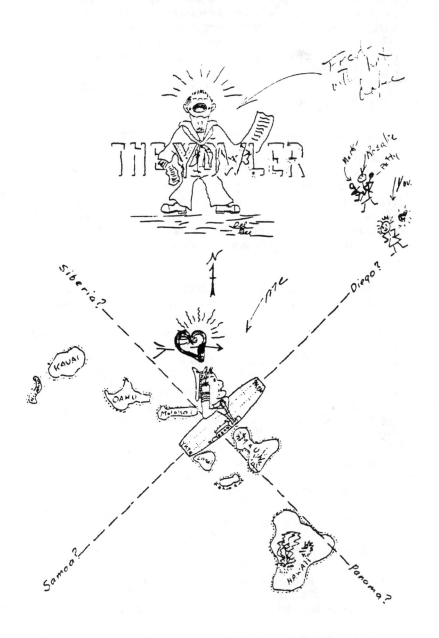

way. *Three officers got leave for San Diego this afternoon, and tonight the admirals sent out radio calls, wires etc trying to reach them, and all leave is canceled. What it means I don't dare guess. Can't believe or depend on any news and never know where we will be the next day.*

We are going into drydock tomorrow and expect to be there for three days.

Bremerton
26 May

Dearest Anne,

Seems certain we will be in San Diego for a couple of days before going back to Hawaii. Some say we will leave from here, but the present schedule unless changed is that we will arrive at the dock at North Island sometime Sunday afternoon or evening and not leave till Wednesday. Oh darling, I must see you if only to hold you in my arms for a minute.

We will get everything all packed and settled when I get home and perhaps have something definite to go on. Let's keep the house for the few days I'm home. I want to be with you in our own little place as long as we can. We will store things when I leave, and you won't have anything but me to worry about, and you can stay with me, or if we get orders to Hawaii, I'll take you with me.

I just can't tell you how much I love you. When is this going to end? I will be crazy all week until I actually hold you in my arms. Nothing is going to go wrong this time. We will crowd a lifetime into a few days. I just hope and pray we will stay a few days longer and if not that it will be over soon and I'll get orders to be based ashore so I can have you with me.

All my love,
Bob

Bremerton
28 May

My darling,

Looks like we will be on schedule at 1100 and Saturday we will be in San Diego til Tuesday, and maybe we don't leave until Wednesday anyhow, will be with you in a few days and what happens afterwards let's not worry about now.

Have the duty tonight and should have a ringside seat for the show coming out of the berth and up the channel.

Will be looking for you on the dock, my darling and throw you a great big kiss. Better wear a football outfit.

38

I'll probably squeeze you to death.
                        Your loving husband

                    # # #

In mid-May Bob got home for three wonderful days. He said
that when he returned to the Yorktown in Hawaii there would be
no way he'd be back unless he was transferred. On the last night
he was home, Bob asked what I'd like him to bring me in case
that happened. Couldn't think of anything but evidently had it
on my mind, because in the middle of the night I sat up straight
in bed and said, "Bring me a piano!" Completely ridiculous since
I can hardly play chopsticks, but when Bob came back, he
brought one—a lovely little Japanese miniature, also two pretty
poorman's pearl necklaces (pukaki shells, white and yellow), and
the tapa cloth that's in the playroom.

After Bob left we settled down to a humdrum existence. The
most exciting event of the week was the arrival of airmail from
Hawaii via the Clipper. It came down from L.A. on Sunday
afternoons and was delivered with the regular mail on Mondays.
Someone had the bright idea of pre-paying 25 cents so the letters
would come special delivery on Sunday evening. This worked
well until everyone found out about it, and the post office was
so flooded with quarters and special delivery requests that it
finally refused to make any further Sunday deliveries.

                    # # #

                Thursday
                4 July
My darling
    *Our dreams are coming true. Before I go any further
and because I'm so excited and will probably rave all over
the place, I want you to be sure to know why I'm happy.
It's not because of Squantum or transfer or going to
Massachusetts or leave or anything like that but because
I'm coming back to you.*

    *My orders read to be detached in July, proceed to
duty NRAB, Squantum, Massachusetts. Fifteen days leave
plus travel time of about seven days. Not too hopeful of
early release from Yorktown as the new fellows haven't yet
qualified (for carrier landings), but they are scheduled to
the 18th. Lexington leaves the 22nd and hope will be sent
on it. Don't get hopes too high, darling, but will be home
inside a month unless something awful happens.*

    *Haven't quite quieted down enough to think things out
but will try to decide about either driving our car or
turning it in on a new one in Detroit and taking a train.*

                        39

Anyway, I won't decide anything until we talk it all over together. Will try so hard to get on my way immediately.

> *Good night, my darling,*
> *sweet dreams,*
> *I love you*

> *Friday*
> *5 July*

Sweetheart,

All day I have been living in the clouds knowing you had my telegram and at last I could send you some good news.

In a few more days I'll be coming home to you, and our life will be like Heaven. Are you happy? Do you want to go to Boston? Will you be happy there? It is one of my ambitions ever since I learned to fly to go back and teach young fellows how to as well as I can.

Enough of that. Let's think of our wonderful trip home—our honeymoon trip we didn't take in October. Seeing our families and how proud I will be taking you home to meet my Mother and Dad. Another little home of our own evenings and weekends together.

Tried the whole shooting match of gold braid today and found I'll be detached as soon as the new fellows arrive aboard on the 18th.

While you're waiting, my angel, could you get from the ALA gas coupons and a planned set of road maps for our trip home—whatever route you would like best. No hurry in packing etc. but be thinking of it for when I arrive there will be only a day or two for everything. Seems, my darling, I'm always leaving you to do the dirty work.

Tomorrow, Anne, is our ninth (month) anniversary. Hope it will be the last one we are apart. I love you more each one that passes.

> *Your loving husband,*

> *18 July*

My darling wife,

I have my orders for transportation back on the Lexington leaving 0700 the 15th, but they will be canceled if Green fails to qualify in the 18th. If he qualifies I'll move to Lexington that very day.

It's wonderful to know that it is only a few days to go before we will be with each other with so much happiness ahead. My hopes are so far ahead my poor old brain and body can't keep up.

Hate to leave Tommy and Wo, Betty and Al, Fergie and Betty and all our friends and all the places we had

*such good times. It's a small world, though, and we will
meet again and often.*

*Squadron let Tommy McKnight and me have our
annual dogfight Monday in honor of my departure, and at
20,000 feet we almost tore each other apart. Gosh, we had
fun. Zoomed everything, stunted and just acted like kids
in Pensacola. We dive bombed the Wariposa as it came in,
but luckily we didn't get reported.*

*Have my last hop in the morning. Turn in my gear
and hope for the best. Don't even fly aboard Thursday
with the other but get to ride the carrier as a guest for the
last time. Transfer to the Lex at anchorage outside of the
harbor.*

*Goodnight, sweet dreams. I am way up in the clouds
and can think only of you.*

Bob

# # #

On a Monday morning in early June we each had a letter,
and came to life again. Tom's letter said the Lex was coming
back to San Diego to be based there for a while. Bob's said that
he had received orders to Squantum (outside Boston) and to be
an instructor, which meant he'd be based ashore and we could
settle down to normal living again. He was coming back on the
Lexington with Tom, and then we'd drive across the country. We
had a '37 Ford Sedan which wasn't in the best shape and Bob
didn't think it could make it all the way. He told me to turn it in
for a newer and better car; he had more faith in me than I had
in myself. I didn't then and still don't know anything about cars,
and the salesmen saw me coming. Each one had a different pitch,
trying to talk me into "surprising my husband with a nice red
convertible" or something similar. I had sense enough not to fall
for that, and decided it would be much smarter to wait and let
Bob pick the car out himself.

The day we'd been living for finally arrived. Tom got in
about two hours ahead of Bob, as he flew his plane in, while Bob
had to wait on board ship until it docked at North Island. Tom
said Bob had told him to tell me to stay at the house and he'd
call as soon as he came ashore. So I waited, and I waited, and I
waited. Finally the phone rang and I heard the sentence that
seemed to haunt us through the next five years: "Where in hell
have you been?" I'd forgotten that Tom had a sadistic sense of
humor. Bob had told him to tell me to meet him dockside, but
Tom thought it extremely funny to tell me I was to wait at home
until Bob called.

Bob had 30 days leave before he had to report in at
Squantum, and he was in such a hurry to drive across country,

41

see his family and find us a place to live that he decided to take a chance on the old car. In the ten months we'd been married we had acquired only a few household goods, mostly wedding presents. In a Navy town it was easier to rent furnished than unfurnished, so we were able to pack all our possessions in the back of the car. We left Coronado on the morning of Bob's birthday, July 29, looking rather like an Okie family in reverse but so happy to be together and have the prospect of not being separated again. Bob's four years would be up the following year and he planned to settle down as a civilian in New England. So much for the plans of mice and men!

Things went well the first morning on the road. We headed north and east through Baker, which was then mainly a gas station, and started up a long slope to the first mountain range we had to cross. About a mile up the engine suddenly died. Bob could find nothing wrong, so came to the conclusion it had to be vapor lock. Fortunately the road was straight so Bob could push the car around, and we started coasting back down toward Baker. The speed of the car finally blew out the air bubble so we turned around and tried the hill again; and this time we made it.

There was no air conditioning for ordinary cars, and as driving across the desert was uncomfortably hot in mid-summer, the AAA suggested that we drive at night. We had dinner in Las Vega, and you'd never believe what it was like then, no neon lights, no gambling casinos, no wedding chapels, no honky tonk at all—just a nice old fashioned town in Nevada. After dinner we drove through the desert, and even then it was hot and sticky. Our destination was Littlefield, Arizona, which according to the AAA had a population of six but a very nice motel. We were a little apprehensive about it, but when we arrived around midnight, we found literally an oasis in the desert. It was a delightful, air-conditioned place, quiet and comfortable. The proprietor and employees of the motel made up the town's population.

We started out very refreshed the next morning, but it seemed as though we spent the first four days going up one side of a mountain and down the other. We were going downhill when Bob noticed that the oil gauge was on 'empty'. He turned off the motor and we coasted downhill to a gas station very conveniently located at the bottom of the hill. We solved that problem by taking a case of oil with us, and adding a quart every hundred miles.

The next afternoon we had just left Salt Lake City and were again going up a mountain when vapor lock struck again, this time on a narrow, windy road. It was difficult and scary trying to turn the car around, but we finally managed it. I might note in passing that the motels were all marvelous in the west, but the farther east we got the lousier they became. Lots of them were

At Bob's Uncle's ranch in Wyoming-Summer of 1940: I'm a pseudo cowgirl. Straddling the fence is as close as I ever got to riding one of their range-wise ponies.

just furnished cabins, and it amused me that in really rural areas they proudly advertised "Simmons mattresses and flush toilets".

Though I was not enthusiastic about it, we planned to stop off for a couple of days to visit Bob's uncle Al Russell and family. (This was the uncle who had visited us when we were first married, and I had invited them to dinner with disastrous results). They had a cattle ranch outside of Wheatland, Wyoming, so we headed there from Salt Lake City. Along the way we drove through the Painted Desert. It was very flat and the altitude quite high, and we were zooming merrily along when suddenly the motor quit—same old vapor lock and no hills to coast down. We sat there a while before a car stopped and reluctantly agreed to give us a push. It was a strange feeling being propelled along the highway faster and faster. Just as our motor caught there was a terrible grinding noise but it was his car, not ours. We couldn't stop for fear we'd never get started again. We felt badly about this, but not badly enough to stop.

Uncle Al's ranch was beautiful, high up in the hills outside of Wheatland, with lots of rolling land, hills and trees. We never saw any cattle, as they were up in the hills for the summer. Surprisingly they had no electricity, just gas lamps and a windmill to pump the water. Bob enjoyed seeing his relatives and it really was a nice rest for us for a few days.

From there we headed toward Chicago along very flat and dusty roads. We spent one night outside of Grand Isle, Nebraska, at an overnight place listed by the AAA, but apparently no one had checked it out. It proved to be one of those places on the outskirts of town where they preferred to rent by the hour rather than by the night. It was noisy all night, but our cabin looked out over a meadow which was lovely by moonlight, and from which came a delightfully cool breeze. The following afternoon we were skirting Chicago, with Bob napping while I drove. Bob had taught me to check the instruments on the dashboard, and when I glanced at them, I noticed that the needle on the generator wasn't registering. I poked Bob and asked if it meant anything, and it did—it meant we had no battery.

We drove to the nearest town, Kendallville, Indiana, and registered at its one hotel, a very seedy one. It must have been on the direct route to the east coast, as there was a Bank of America travelers' check tacked to the wall back of the desk. At that time Bank of America was a local California bank, and we'd been skeptical about using their checks for fear they wouldn't be honored away from the west. However, Bob decided there was no point in spending more money on our poor little car, so off we went to the town's one Ford agency. We were looking for what was known as a business coupe with just a front seat and a large area for storage. They didn't have that model so we hiked to the Chevy agency, and there in the showroom was a shiny green business coupe. Our problem was what to use for cash, since we had no credit rating and it was 6 o'clock on a Saturday night. However, we gave them the name of the bank manager in Coronado and also Bob's dad's name, and they said they'd see what arrangements could be made, and would let us know on Sunday morning. We spent a, to say the least, restless night. The uncertainty about the car for one thing, but more than that, Kendallville was on the direct route between New York City and Chicago and the hotel itself was right on the tracks. Seemed as if there were trains every ten minutes, and every time they went by there was a great roar and an accompanying rattle of bed and chandelier. We never did find out how they established our credit rating. Bob's dad said they didn't call him. About 9 a.m. on Sunday they called and said to come get our new car—the price, as I recall, was around $796. So over we went, transferred our worldly possessions to our new, shiny green car, and took off. What a delightful feeling not to have to worry about vapor lock, leaking oil, or dying batteries. Had we been stopped by the police we would have been in trouble: no registration, just a bill of sale; Indiana dealers' plates, and California drivers' licenses. I had a coke as we drove along and couldn't finish it so Bob said to toss the half-full bottle out of the window—(in 1940 the word littering was unheard of.) I threw it so carelessly that the liquid flew back in the window all over the shiny new dashboard. Bob was upset, and my name was mud the rest of the afternoon. But we had no more problems and finally reached our destination, Bob's home in East Longmeadow, Massachusetts, weary from our long journey.

The closer we got to Bob's home the more excited he became, and the more apprehensive I got. I'd never met his family and didn't know how they felt about me, but was sure there were a few strikes against me from the start. Bob and I had gone together for such a short time before we were married, in contrast to his older brother Russ and his wife Sis. Then Bob hadn't let them know we were getting married until it was a fait accompli. And I felt I'd never pass the test as a proper New England housewife, and although the first time Bob's mother and I were alone she informed me that she had cried for three days after receiving the telegram Bob sent her from Warner's Hot Springs telling of our marriage, perhaps that got the resentment out of her system. They seemed glad to see us and made us welcome. We stayed for a few days, then took off for Boston to find a place to live that would be near Squantum where Bob would be stationed. My Aunt Edith lived in Weymouth and my cousins, Nat and Mary Clapp, in Hingham and I wanted to stay with them. But Russ and Sis lived in Framingham and Bob's mother said they'd never forgive us if we didn't stay with them, so that's what we did.

Finding a furnished house to rent was more difficult around Boston than in small Navy towns, where much of the town's income came from renting to Navy couples. Finally we found a funny little house in Wollaston, just about five minutes from the base and very convenient. If I had the car, Bob would quite often zoom the house and waggle the wings of his little yellow training plane, a signal for me to come and pick him up.

Chapter 4

That winter was a lovely time for us, even though the situation abroad kept getting more and more tense. There were a number of young couples attached to the base and our social life was very gay, in the old-fashioned sense of the word.

This was my first real winter in New England—of course, I had spent four years in Northampton while I was at Smith, but dorm life was completely different, and I wasn't aware of the cold and snow unless it interfered with a social engagement. I have lived her now for over forty years but still don't like snow and am convinced each year when winter comes that we will be snowbound at least once—it hasn't happened ever, but I still dread the thought and each winter lay in a supply of food in case it does.

We weren't used to heating bills, either and were a little worried that we would be unable to keep up with our oil bill. Oil was 7 cents a gallon which we thought so horrendous that we only heated the downstairs and the bathroom upstairs (which was so antiquated the toilet tank was overhead with a long pull chain for flushing). On really cold nights we would undress in the bathroom, open the door, take a fast run and jump into bed. Ah, the hot blood of youth.

One morning in November I had a new experience. I hung our laundry out in the back yard. It was chilly, and my hands felt like lumps of ice, but I was sure the clothes would be dry and fluffy when I took them in—even though they were washed and wrung by hand and rather drippy when I hung them out.

I was away until late afternoon, and when I came home and rushed out to take the aforementioned laundry down, I was quite puzzled to find it all stiff as a board. I couldn't figure out why (thought, perhaps, I hadn't rinsed the soap out). I left it on the kitchen table and went off to pick up Bob. Much to my amazement when I got back the clothes were a soggy mess and water was trickling across the floor. My first experience with the fact that oftentimes in New England the temperature stayed below 32 degrees all day, and anything left outside would freeze.

Another day when Bob had the 24 hour duty, I discovered to my dismay that the drain pipe from the kitchen sink was clogged. I worked at it for two days with plunger and Drano but got nowhere. The first thing that Bob did when he got home that night was to go down to the cellar to investigate—without changing out of his uniform. He found where the trouble was, but, unfortunately while he was fooling around with that section of pipe, it disintegrated in his hands covering his uniform with grease and drano. We were able to find a dry cleaner still open who saved Bob's greens from destruction, but we couldn't locate a plumber so Bob improvised by connecting the two pieces of

Bob as instructor at Squantum, September 1940 to June 1942.

pipe with a section of inner tube, and so it remained all the rest of the time we were there. (The landlady had promised to send a plumber but never did.)

I spent a goodly portion of my time worrying about Bob when he was out flying or when he didn't appear on time at places where he was supposed to be, but my whereabouts never gave him any visible concern at all. Of course, his occupation was slightly more hazardous than mine which must have had some bearing on the above facts.

One morning I dropped Bob off at the base and drove up to spend the day with Russ and Sis in Framingham having promised to pick him up at 4 p.m. I left there in plenty of time, but on the way back I ran into a thunderstorm of such intensity that it caused mini-floods here and there—one of which I had to go through in the Wellesly underpass on Route 9. In my ignorance I thought the best way to get through it was to go as fast as I could so that, naturally, the splashing water killed the motor, and I had to sit there for over an hour until the coils dried out sufficiently to restart the motor. At first I was upset over causing Bob worry but then I thought, "No. Maybe now he'll appreciate what I go through all too frequently."

As soon as I got back to Wollaston I drove hurriedly to the base some hour and a half late only to have the Marine on duty there tell me that Ensign McCullough had left a message for me that he had gotten a ride home. Feeling surer than ever (and a little gloatingly) that he would be upset because I had the only house key I went quickly home. Wrong again. Bob had jimmied the kitchen window and was upstairs happily singing in the shower. He never even commented on my tardiness. I was in high dungeon the rest of the evening. He could at least have showed me the courtesy of asking where in hell I had been.

Just about a month before Bob's four years would have been up, the President declared a national emergency, and no one was to be released from the service until it was over, which proved to be some five years later. For us those five years were filled with joy, sorrow, frustration; also indecision, fulfillment, and uncertainties. Name an emotion and it happened to us, as it did to everyone in the armed forces.

We re-acquired Willie that fall in Wollaston. He was my English Cocker I had left with my father when I went to the west coast in the summer of 1937. My father was then living with my aunt, who was ruining the dog by spoiling him completely, and my father wanted us to take him. My aunt didn't want to lose him, and when we took him she cut us out of her will, a habit she had with her four nieces when anyone did something against her wishes. We were in and out of her will several times, but luckily happened to be in when she finally departed this world.

As a point of interest, Joe Kennedy Jr. went through Squantum while Bob was instructing. Although he wasn't Bob's student, Bob was instrumental in his getting through basic training and subsequently acquiring his wings as Naval Aviator. He was having such a problem with air sickness on his early morning training flights that he was about to wash out. Bob discovered Joe's breakfast always consisted of cold cereal and milk and told him that if he would switch to a hot meal the problem would right itself. He did, and it did. I don't suppose the Kennedy's would have thanked Bob for what he did, but then I always felt the Kennedy boys were doomed no matter what.

In the summer of 1941 Bob started having spells of upset stomach. The base doctor (in civilian life an eye, ear, nose and throat man) prescribed milk of magnesia, which resulted in worse pain. Since the Navy doctor lived on the north side of Boston, we called in a civilian doctor who, with one poke, diagnosed appendicitis. He thought it was subsiding but said if it got worse to call him immediately, and I called that morning around 2 a.m. The doctor had been called to the scene of an accident at Fore River Shipyard but his wife promised to send him as soon as he returned, which was about 9 a.m. When he came he was afraid the appendix might have ruptured and wanted to get Bob to the hospital immediately, but we ran into another snag. Since Bob was in the service he couldn't go to a civilian hospital without a release from the Navy, and the skipper of Squantum was on leave. The exec wasted a couple of hours trying to decide whether he had authority for the release. Finally decided he didn't, but sent an ambulance to take Bob to the Chelsea Naval Hospital, miles away on the other side of Boston. Bob said it was a terrible trip—the young corpsman drove hell bent for leather with siren wide open, over cobblestones and in and out of el columns straight up Atlantic Avenue. When they got to the hospital, the elevator was stuck between floors on the way to the operating room for half an hour. Finally they removed his appendix, fortunately in time.

Bob was in the hospital for three weeks, and I drove up every day to spend the afternoon with him. I was always caught in a huge traffic jam going home through Charlestown and Boston. About the last day Bob was there it dawned on me that I could have avoided this by leaving 15 minutes earlier and avoiding the thousands of cars that converged on the Charlestown bridge as the Navy Yard day shift was getting out. Bob had a month's leave to recuperate and it was a lovely, relaxing time.

Soon after this I had to go to Washington because my father had sadly concluded he couldn't keep the house alone and was putting it on the market. Wo and I had just three days to decide what household furnishings we wanted to keep, and even now I think of things I wish we hadn't let go. We should have had three years to make all those decisions. When I got back and told Bob about the furniture we began to look for an unfurnished house, and finally found one in Hingham with six rooms. It was in a housing development, but the houses were all different, with big yards and trees. We moved in September 1941, and that's where we were when the Japanese bombed Pearl Harbor on December 7. Who can ever forget what he or she was doing that cold Sunday afternoon, the 7th of December, when the announcement came over the radio? We were having a very domestic and puttery day. I was in the living room trying to make myself think I was enjoying doing some necessary mending, and Bob was down in the cellar rewiring a broken lamp. I don't think we ever finished those two particular tasks. All the rest of the day and night we seemed frozen in time like the figures in a glass paperweight the moment before it is inverted and they are enveloped in a maelstrom of snow. For the next four years, when Bob left the house in the morning I never knew whether he'd be back that night or be gone for six months or longer. The whole country was in a state of confusion, and I was slightly pregnant. Anne was a Pre-Pearl Harbor baby by six days. Everyone was being transferred like crazy, but Bob stayed at Squantum for 5½ precious months.

One Saturday in June Bob said he had Sunday off, which seemed strange since everyone worked seven days a week. He arranged to play golf with two old friends from Springfield, whose wives were going to keep me company. As Bob grabbed his clubs and went out the door he said "I've been ordered to Seattle to the escort carrier Bogue and have to report in in two weeks." Then off he went, leaving me completely stunned, trying to be a good hostess while mentally packing and storing so I could go with him. Of course he wouldn't take me and the doctor wouldn't let me go, but that didn't make me any happier. Seattle was jammed, no housing available or hospital beds. So I saw him off and resigned myself to three months of incubating with Willie to keep me company.

When Bob got to Seattle the Bogue hadn't even been commissioned, and he and Joe Byros were the only members of the fighter squadron to have arrived. They were leading a very cushy life with not much to do except play golf and go fishing. The monotony was broken by an air raid alert. It was reported that the Japs were about to attack Seattle as they had Pearl Harbor. As the only fighter pilots available, Bob and Joe were sent up to defend the city in a couple of unarmed fighter planes! Bob said it was a really hairy feeling, but fortunately it was a false alarm and they came down in one piece.

# # #

VGS 9
N.A.S. Air Station, Seattle, Wash.
2 June, 1942

My dearest wife,

Gosh how terrible it is to be away from you. I'm lonesome and miss you more than anything in the world.

Think it swell of the Harveys and Russ and Sis to see me off and drive the car home for you. Arrived in Springfield and what a delegation to see me go through . . . Mother and Dad and ten neighbors and relatives. Everyone brought me presents.

Had a swell stop over in Chicago with Betty and Al. Both just the same, and how good it was to see them. Really felt blue after I left them. I guess up until then I hadn't lost all hold on our life together

Arrived in Seattle right on time, and Joe Byros was there with the big red car and two side boys for my bags. Caused quite a stir with the other fellows on the train. You know Joe had to have a big show . . . Everything worked as smooth as a whistle. All bags okay and flight gear, too. Get travel money Monday and will send it home to you as my base pay came today and is plenty to keep me going.

Checked in O.K., and I'm the skipper for the time being—Joe—the exec. We have four F-4-F's—forty-seven enlisted men. We start flying in the morning. F-4-F looks good. Quite anxious to get started.

The station here is too beautiful to describe. B.O.Q. is a palace, Joe and I have two rooms and a bath. Big stuffed furniture and better than any hotel room I was ever in. Civilian room service. No officers' mess but regular dining hall—waitresses, menus, etc.

Outside my window is the first green of the station golf course and in between all rose gardens. I can reach out and pick ten different kinds—very beautiful. I've never seen such a bar. It's the screwiest but swankiest place you can imagine. North Island, Squantum and Pensacola are just outhouses in comparison.

Station is so darned big if it weren't for Joe's car we would be lost. Seattle is about ten miles from the station which is on a big lake about ten miles from anywhere.

This being away from you is the hardest thing I have every faced. Take awfully good care of yourself and Junior. Gosh, I hope I'm home to be with you in August.

I love you so,
Bob

VGS 9
N.A.S. Seattle, Wash.
June 6, 1943

Dearest Anne,

Just received two grand letters from you, and it's wonderful to hear. The mail gets kicked around here somewhat. Gosh, it's nice to know everyone is taking such good care of you and Junior and Willie, and I don't have to worry so much as if you were all alone. Nice to think of you at home, and I can imagine how everything is placed and what you are doing and even guess how the sweetpeas are coming.

I only wish I could say come on out, but really it is quite bad here as you must know after Dutch Harbor. We've been on alert for the past few days. I only missed going up there by two days. Joe and I are pretty well along in the fighters and stand a continuous patrol in the defense of the Air Station. They are swell planes—quite hard to handle and awfully fast but quite a delight after Squantum.

I stood my first watch last night and for Joe, by the way. It's a humdinger and suited for about a Lt. Cdr. and above. Com Air Task Group of the northwest of the U.S. Twenty-four watch one in four. Very exciting. We know all about everything and only wish I could tell you. Not very good news, anyway do you see why I cant have you out here.

Not much news about the ship—no planes of our own yet so should be here a while if not sent to Dutch Harbor.

I live for the day when we are together again, and we'll have our whole lives together. No Navy to worry about for at least twenty years.

Keep your chin up, sweetie. I love you.

Bob

June 14

Darling Anne,

Just another rainy night in Seattle. Didn't do anything today. Slept until noon with an awful hangover from last night. Sat around the bar until about 0200 with Joe and the boys and sort of drowned our sorrows and paid for it today.

Our skipper is a Lt. Cdr. Drone and a swell fellow. There's always one bastard in every squadron—ours is our exec. Lt. Rogers. He is pretty nasty, eager and mean—already we hate the sight of him and call him "Squeaky".

The wives seem nice and friendly. They're all sorry

about your not being here. So far they haven't been able to get houses, and a couple of them are living in tourist camps. They don't seem to want to rent out here, but insist on people buying the house.

Sure miss you, darling. Goodnight and sweet dreams.

> *I love you,*
> *Bob*

8 June

Darling,

Haven't written since Wednesday and debating whether or not to send a telegram but decided against not knowing if it would scare you or might arrive in the night.

Had dinner with a doctor and wife from Boston and Springfield. Kind of silly. Went down to the city hospital with him on emergency and didn't get home until late. What a lousy hospital, and they don't have doctors or interns enough so the Navy Doc goes down when they get in trouble. People have to have their babies at home it's that bad. Invited me to go with him some night on a delivery, but I said "No way!"

Remember reading about Winchell and the sub shelling the coast here? well, I had the watch and was first to get the report and had to organize etc. and put all the wheels in action. It gets pretty rough on watch and glad to get off.

No sign of planes yet. If we had them wouldn't be surprised if we didn't go to Alaska right away ship or no ship.

Read where the gas business is getting worse. I hope you can still keep the B3 card. If they ask you, tell them I'm still there. I am in spirit.

Are you feeling okay? It's awful not being able to take care of you as I want to.

> *I love you,*
> *Bob*

2 July

Darling,

May and June gone over the hill. Hard to realize it's almost the Fourth. Had I been home I was going to set off such loud firecrackers in celebration of our love for each other. Just another working day here.

Damn, but it's hot. Same yesterday and not a breath of air—113 degrees. Just a couple of days ago we were wearing greens. Look out the window and see the snow on the mountains—what a joke. Have on bottom of pajamas and soaking right through so I guess I sleep raw tonight as I do at home.

*Went in town yesterday looking for a cribbage board.
I want to get us a carved ivory walrus tusk. Asked a
policeman where to go and he said, "Hell, come to my
house and I'll give you mine." "Been in the family for 20
years." It came from Alaska and was made by Eskimos.*

*Sure healthy but not very happy. Love you, my darling
and miss you more every day.*

# # #

Willie and I got along fine through July and part of August
though life was so uneventful during that period that the only
happening I remember was one that nearly cost me Willie and the
baby too. Across the grassy mall that separated the back of our
house from that of our neighbors on the next street lived a Pit
Bull—typically, gentle to humans but death to any other animal.
He was always kept chained in the same place by their back
door, and Willie, on his daily peregrinations, knew exactly how
close he could come to the dog and still stay beyond the length
of it's tether.

I let him out one morning and went about my hapless little
household chores when suddenly I realized he had been gone
much longer than usual. I looked out the back window, and to
my horror there was Willie spread-eagled on the ground with the
Pit Bull standing over him jaws poised at his throat. His owners
had evidently moved him from the back door to the edge of the
garage, and Willie, not being aware of this, had nonchalantly
strolled into the incipient jaws of death. I watched panic stricken
for what seemed like an eternity. Willie moved not so much as a
hair not did the other dog. Finally I pulled myself together
sufficiently to phone the dog's owners who were evidently
unaware of what was going on. I couldn't watch because I was
afraid the slightest movement would cause the Pit Bull to bury
his fangs in Willie's throat. However, they must have had
remarkable control because in a few minutes Willie came
crawling home trembling, covered with dirt and with that awful
smell of utter fear about him. It took us several days to recover
from our horrible experience. Thank goodness, Willie learned his
lesson and ever after skirted that yard by a goodly margin.
Thank goodness, too, I suffered no ill effects though along with
Willie I shook for the remainder of the morning.

# # #

*Officers Mess
Naval Air Station
Seattle, Washington*

5 August, 1942

My darling,

My day off. Feels good. Missed my last one due to ferrying a plane to Sitka, an 032N-1.

Finally got started on our flight to Alaska about 1400 the 30th. Made two 300 mile legs and then stayed overnight at a Canadian base, Coal Harbor. Pretty wild country and all mountains and big trees and lots of water. Landed at a Canadian base on Alleford Bay a way off in the mountains on an island. Had supper, gassed up and then pushed on.

The Canadians are swell, and first thing they did was to push a drink into your hand. Got in just at dark and just like landing in a saucer. They picked us up in little motor boats, and it was dark before we got ashore—about 2200, I guess. Had drinks and a midnight supper and fun. Left there about 0800 had got to Sitka about 1200. They didn't have any way to get us home so had to stay until Monday until a big boat came and brought us back.

Had a swell time in Sitka—mostly an Indian town and quite rugged. The fellows on duty there raise hell every night. Gamble every night and drink like fish. All the wives were shipped out when the war started. BOQ quite nice and fairly comfortable. The Canadian places are just like boys' summer camp. Saw lots of Eskimos and their villages and totem poles, and a fish packing company which was interesting aside from its smell.

Saw some cribbage boards that were honeys but cost like the dickens. Fifty dollars, and I was too tight to part with that.

Had a swell trip back in a PBY—on instruments most of the time. Would surely like to take you on a boat ride to Alaska after the war. Its really a beautiful country.

Be careful, darling, you are getting close now and miss you and love you,

Bob

# # #

One night I woke up with some strange pains, so I betook myself up to Norwood to stay with Russ and Sis. Sis was pregnant too, and her baby was due three weeks after mine. We speculated what would happen if they came at the same time; she was going to Framingham, 21 miles west, and I to Quincy, 18 miles in the opposite direction. Fortunately they awaited their respective terms. Poor Russ—he'd take the two of us to dinner, and people would smile as we walked down the street, he with not one but two females each looking as if she'd swallowed a

56

watermelon.

\# \# \#

7 August

My sweetheart,
    It's a bit late. Been to a USO show starring Bing Crosby and the troupe. Everyone ended up at the CC Club bar. Good time.
    Could you maybe send me a wire a day or two before the baby comes. Ask Dr. Van Raalte if he could call it that close. I'd then be able to hop a plane. Otherwise hate to take 14 days leave, then have you hold out on us all and I have to leave before I know you are all right. Otherwise I'll wait until the baby arrives then hop for home and be with you as soon as I can.

I love you
Bob

\# \# \#

My doctor was due to go into the army on September 3rd, and wanted my baby here before he left. We tried doses of castor oil which didn't work, so on August 31, 1942, I went to the hospital and labor was induced. They gave me nembutol and I remember nothing about my delivery, just woke up next morning and there was Anne, a cute little blue-eyed doll with lots of long black hair and no name because we expected a boy. Russ sent a telegram to Bob, who sent one back saying he was glad the waiting was over, and I settled down to two weeks of recuperating in the hospital. At that time the cost of a private room was $7 a day, which included everything; choice of menu, all the comforts of home. I was the only private patient in maternity and my room became a social center for the nurses, life was as pleasant as it could be with no proud papa around.

\# \# \#

Seattle
1 September

My darling,
    So excited. Have been that way all last night and today. Suppose there are millions of things all new papas are supposed to do, but, darn, I'm just so numb haven't done anything. Been in a regular daze.
    Telegram arrived about 1800 our time. Had just

57

finished supper. Darned fellows got me so full of drinks I
couldn't do anything. Knew I couldn't reach you until
morning. Can hardly wait until I hear from you and all
about the baby. The telegram says nothing except she
arrived at 7:30 p.m., a nice sweet girl and you were all
right.
　　　Gave out about thirty cigars today and had lots of
handshakes.
　　　What wouldn't I give to be home with you, my sweet. I
wouldn't have had you go through this alone for anything
if I could have helped it. Trying so hard to get things
squared so I can come home to you, but seem to get
nowhere.

I love you
Bob

# # #

One morning about a week after Anne was born I was
reading the newspaper when a nurse came in and started
straightening up my room. She told me to comb my hair and put
on some lipstick as there was a visitor in uniform outside. Russ
had been talking about entering the service, and I thought he had
come to show me how he looked, but I dutifully fixed myself up
a bit. The nurse opened the door with a flourish and to my
amazement and delight there stood Bob, with a gigantic plush
pink rabbit whose nether regions were encased in diapers,
mercifully concealed by a large paper bag given him by a kind
stewardess. He had emergency leave, and the squadron had given
him a congratulatory party and poured him on the plane, foisting
the rabbit on him as he boarded. He said the damned thing
gurgled all the way across the country. He tried to leave it on the
plane and even on a bench during a long layover in Chicago but
it was still there when he got back to the airport. So he brought
it the last lap and shook it out of the bag onto my bed. The
diaper held all sorts of things: pacifiers, pins, a lovely hand-
embroidered pink silk kimono for Anne—and the gurgle turned
out to be a bottle of Haig & Haig, much more expensive than we
could afford. We kept it for the rest of the war, and opened it on
VJ Day in Corpus Christi.
　　　When Bob got to the hospital, Anne was still known only as
Baby McCullough because I felt I couldn't make as important a
decision as a name without him and had no word on the subject.
We had a conclave, and he wanted to name her Anne which I
thought would end up by our being respectively Big Anne and
Little Anne so we solved that and thought we had also killed two
birds with one stone by naming her Anne Frances. Bob's

58

Anne and proud parents in Hingham, September 1942.

Mother's name was Frances and I had a great aunt, Annie Frances, after whom I had been named. We thought thus to mollify both sides of the family—but not so. She is still known to my family as Anne Frances, but Bob's family had an aversion to double names and wouldn't call her thusly. So since I was around them a great deal of the time, I became Big Anne after all.

Bob had to go back the day after I got home from the hospital. It would have been the day before if I hadn't flouted routine and the doctors orders. The doctor who delivered Anne departed for the Army three days after she was born and left me in the care of a charming elderly doctor who had retired but then came back to help plug the ranks decimated by the various services. He hadn't handled an obstetrical case in thirty years and seemed to be petrified of me. For a routine pelvic exam he would have the nurse drape the sheet gracefully and strategically around me, and then he stood in the doorway peering in my direction. Even forty years younger and with perfect vision I think he would have found the view somewhat indistinct. As I think I said before the routine stay in the maternity wing was fourteen days which meant I would be leaving the day Bob had to leave, too. The doctor obstinately refused to release me a minute earlier so finally I, just as obstinately, said I was leaving a day earlier, anyway—which I did. Up to the present moment I have never been able to ascertain that my one day early abdication from my hospital bed was at all injurious to my health, and it did give me 24 more precious hours with Bob.

My aunt called to ask if she could spend the night on her way home from Vermont. When I asked if she could wait until the next night so Bob and I could be alone (except for Anne, Willie, and Anne's nurse, Miss Ellis) she got so insulted that she cut us out of her will once again.

21 September

My darling,

We are still in Seattle but expect to go to San Diego Wed. for about a week for refresher landings on some carrier. They push us around so and confuse us so that we don't know anything. I figure we'll be at sea about the middle of October. Sure glad you're settled comfortably at home and not out here trying to outguess Uncle Sam and worrying about being left in some dump waiting for us to come back.

Squadron about the same even though somewhat confused. I managed to get home during the only period I could have possibly gotten leave. It's absolutely out of the question now things are popping so. We were surely lucky. Golly, it was so wonderful. I'm still wondering how it all happened.

Might have some more news in a day or two. Anyway,
I'll let you know when I arrive in San Diego.
                    I love you
                    Bob

                    Hotel Del Coronado
                    Coronado, Calif.
                    27 Sept. Sunday
My darling,
   Golly, how lonesome it is here without you, sweetie.
Everything holds so many wonderful memories for us.
Walked down the beach to our old bench and watched the
waves breaking. A beautiful night—just that little haze so
the lights look fuzzy. The waves so big and so loud. No
one around but you and me. Every wave meant days, and I
wondered when I would ever be back to you for good.
   We left Seattle Friday by plane. Stayed in Frisco
overnight. Had a grand time. The base there is quite swell.
We got as far as L.A. Saturday afternoon and then took a
bus to San Diego. Arrived quite late and tired. No rooms
anywhere, and I finally stole a fellows bed and had a hell
of a row about 0100 when he came home, but I won out.
Tonight we have rooms here at the hotel and will until we
head back. Got to get up at 0600 and go out on carrier if
weather is good. Haven't any idea how long we'll be here
but less than a week, anyway.
   Miss your letters but will have them all when I get
back.
                    How I love you,
                    Bob

                    Hotel Del Coronado
                    3 October
My darling wife,
   I guess this will reach you about on our wedding
anniversary and wish we could have been together. We love
each other so and have been so happy together. Seems as
if we have been married three days not three years. This
may have been a bad year for us but chin up and we'll be
together soon.
   Didn't get to leave Coronado—maybe in the morning.
The rest won't, but I am waiting to fly a new fighter up.
Don't think our new base will be very pleasant. When I saw
it last (I was waiting for your plane to come in just
before we were married, remember?) it wasn't much of a
base. However we ought to get lots of flying in and that is
what we need if we are to go out soon. Wonder what
condition I'll find my gear in when they finally bring it

down.

Remember, sweetie, on our third anniversary I love you more than on our first though that's not possible.

Bob

Hotel Del Coronado
2 October FRI

My darling,

Golly, have I lots of bellyaching tonight. We arrived here in Coronado on Saturday night and hung around on call by the planes until Wednesday morning, finally boarding the carrier at 0730. Did nothing out there and finally arrived back Friday night. Only qualified 8 out of thirty. I was one of the eight. Boy, it was pretty bad, and they only dared let us old pilots try it. At times we were flying below the deck coming up the groove it pitched so.

Anyway—the biggest gripe is with all our belongings, bills, mail, etc.—all up in Seattle unattended. They switched our base to San Pedro, and we aren't going back to Seattle. Some one I suppose, packed our gear for us and I hate to think of the mess it will be in.

I feel sorry more for others than I do for myself. Some have their wives there and their cars. Some bought houses. It happened so damn sudden. Sure glad you are safe and sound in our little place in Hingham and don't have to put up with that awful mess. Worries me how we are ever going to win the war. We are no more trained or ready in our squadron than a bunch of school girls. I think I can take care of myself, but the poor new fellows are so terribly green and so eager. I'm afraid lots of them will get hurt.

Pretty mixed up letter but pretty sore tonight and mixed up myself. Will write a nice letter tomorrow and let you know how I like my new quarters.

Sweet dreams
I love you
Bob

p.s. Before I got this sealed along came my gear. A mess is right. Somebody spread a blanket on the floor of my quarters and just dumped everything I own in—clothes, shoes, pictures, books, radio, and then they tied a knot in the blanket and here it is. Everything seems to be here except my little carved ivory idol which was different because it was a hunchback, and the Eskimos only carve what they see. Somebody probably has a unique new knickknack. A perfect ending to a fouled up week.

# # #

Miss Ellis stayed for three weeks, more for companionship than anything else, and I hated to see her go as it was so lonesome. She promised she'd take care of Anne if the time came when Bob would be ashore for a while in San Diego and I cold join him. The opportunity came around the first of November.

I'd been nursing Anne and didn't know how to go about shutting off the supply, but the doctor said it was easy, no liquids for 48 hours and some little red pills. So I packed my clothes, the pills, Anne and Willie and Miss Ellis and took them to Bob's home in East Longmeadow to stay until I got back. Bob's dad got me a plane ticket, drove me to Brainard Field (precursor of Bradley) and I took off about 3 p.m. Flying was a sometime thing during the war years; civilians had no priority and were bumped indiscriminately for servicemen or anyone important.

By the time we got to Pittsburgh I was the only female and only civilian on the plane. We were to touch down in Chicago about 8 p.m. and hopefully I'd still be aboard when we took off for points west. I've always been very literal-minded and when the doctor said to cut out liquids I took him at his word; I had nothing to drink for 24 hours. I was so excited about the trip I smoked a lot, and the combination made me feel as though I'd been in the Sahara for an eternity.

Outside Chicago the air became turbulent, and the plane reversed direction; because of storms we couldn't land in Chicago and headed for Toledo—one step forward, two steps back. The airline put the army officers, the stewardess and me up for the night at a nice hotel, and said the flight would continue in the morning. We were never supposed to know where our husbands were, so I sent Bob a telegram c/o Commandant, Naval District, San Diego, saying I'd be delayed.

I went up to bed with dry throat and parched tongue, and in about ten minutes the phone range. The stewardess and officers had gathered in the bar and invited me to join them. I was too embarrassed to tell them I couldn't because I was trying to stop the flow of basic baby formula and was so thirsty that if I heard one tinkle of ice I'd probably drink everything in sight in two gulps. They were so nice and friendly, and 40 years later I apologize. The next morning the airline called to say they'd put me on a flight to St. Louis and then would work from there. While I was waiting in St. Louis I sent another telegram to Bob, then in mid-afternoon caught a flight to L.A.—as usual, me and a group of servicemen. We arrived in L.A. after dark and found there were no flights to San Diego, but the airline put me up at the Biltmore and promised to get me on a flight in the morning. Before going to bed I sent another telegram to Bob.

Next morning the airport was fogged in, and the best bet

seemed to catch a 9 a.m. train for San Diego. One more telegram, and off I went to Union station with my three suitcases and a few extras, not a problem when flying, but a handicap when trying to get through mobs of people jamming the gates. I think all the porters went into the baggage room and played poker with their tips. I got only halfway to the gates when they were closed, but a loud speaker announced another train at noon. I sent another telegram and sat myself down on my luggage squarely in front of the gates; the area was soon choked with people all with the same purpose. When the gates opened, my luggage and I were swept through; I got in the door of the nearest coach and actually found a seat. As we neared San Diego I began to feel apprehensive, wondering if Bob had received my telegrams and what I'd do if he wasn't there to meet me. When the train finally pulled into the station and I juggled myself and luggage into the mob, there he was, greeting me with our old refrain: "Where in hell have you been?" He'd meet every type of transportation then he'd go back and pick up another telegram.

Bob had very plush quarters at the Hotel Del Coronado but they were strictly B.O.Q., so he found us a room near our old honeymoon duplex. Rooms were almost impossible to get, so despite its drawbacks the room Bob found was Shangri-La to us. The house belonged to a very British woman who had left England with her two sons to escape the blitz. This was her only means of support and she wasted no money on frills, no bedspreads, no rugs, no shade on the one lamp. We were fortunate, though, to have our own bathroom with a lovely big tub. There were three other couples there; one army enlisted man who had a wife and six-month old baby, whose crib was a bureau drawer. I was the luckiest because Bob came home almost every night. Though when Bob left in the morning, I never really knew whether he'd be back that night, that weekend, or not at all.

Chapter 5

It was another idyllic time for Bob and me. We'd have breakfast together and then he'd take off, and the other wives and I would spend the day doing laundry, or walking the beach, or playing with the baby. About 3:30 in the afternoon I'd start looking for Bob to come down the walk. We'd have a drink in our room, then go to L'Avenida for dinner and afterwards to a movie, or back to our room to play acey-deucy and listen to the radio, usually Bob Hope or a Tia Juana station that played recordings banned in the states. They were so mild they wouldn't be noticed today but were considered quite racy in the 40's. Or we would walk over to the ocean through the blackout to our favorite bench atop the breakwater which kept the sea from the town. During those first halcyon months of our marriage when we were living at 959 E Avenue we used to go there quite often in the evenings—sometimes we watched the sunset; sometimes we couldn't even sit on the rocks because the tide was so high and the waves so rough the surf crashed over the breakwater and sent feathers of spray across the road. (Back in the early forties that strip of gold-flecked sand was only about fifty yards wide at low tide so there was very little space for sunning or picnicking, but now the water has receded almost a quarter of a mile, and there is plenty of room for almost anything a beach goer might have had in mind). The best times, though, were when the fog had crept unobtrusively in. The only light was a diffused glow from a nearby street lamp, and we were enclosed in a nebulous velvety world of our own penetrated only by the haunting sound of the Point Loma foghorn (Even the travesty that Lifebuoy soap's commercial had made of it couldn't destroy its poignancy). It was as nearly perfect a time as it could be with the sword of Damocles hanging over our heads in the form of the Empire of Japan.

Bob didn't come home for several nights, including Thanksgiving, so Doris, mother of the baby, and I went to La Avenida for dinner. We insisted on a table for four, pretending our husbands were in the empty seats. Bob came home over the weekend, but said if he didn't show up Monday I might as well head back east to wait for the next break.

With unspeakable sadness I called the airlines and made a tentative reservation for Tuesday. I didn't tell the landlady as I planned to pay for the rest of the week anyway. But she heard me on the phone and was so afraid she'd go one day without rent that she rented our room to another navy couple, starting that night. I was beside myself, no place to lay my weary head and still filled with hope that Bob might miraculously turn up, which of course he didn't. The other wives rallied round and let me have half a bed; no other husbands were home either.

At Sea
Friday
4 December

My darling,
Seems as if the world comes to an end every time we have to part.
From the ship I watched your plane arrive and take off from the airport in San Diego. I waved a kiss goodbye to you. Did you get it? Called Mrs. Harrell so knew you got away O.K. So nice of all the girls to see you off in my place. We had to stay aboard but didn't leave until early next morning and have been out ever since. Fog pretty thick both Tues. and Wed. mornings.
Your telegram hadn't arrived by 1100 Wednesday so had to leave not knowing whether you arrived in Washington or not. Surely anxious to hear all about Anne. Be sure to write me all the little details.
My address probably for a short time will be the same, but if we leave, it becomes:
   VGS-9
   U.S.S. Bogue
   c/o Fleet Post Office
   San Francisco, Calif.
Been flying quite steadily now and long hours. Maybe getting into port sometime tomorrow. Will be quite uneasy until I hear how you are and if the trip was o.k.
Golly, it was so wonderful being with you again if only for a short time. Flight quarters at dawn so I had better hit the sack.
> *Goodnight and sweet dreams*
> *I love you*
> *Bob*

# # #

So the next day I unwillingly left Coronado and headed back east. The airlines said I was cleared as far as Dallas, and were sure I'd be cleared to Washington from there, so I boarded the plane not very cheerfully but with no premonition of what lay ahead. Fortunately I sat next to a Marine wife who was also going to Washington, and who had been sold the same bill of goods by the airline. Her name was Becky McIntyre. I'd never seen her before and have never seen her since, but if she hadn't happened along I might still be sitting in the Dallas airport, mummified and covered with dust. When we landed in Dallas we went to the reservation desk to pick up the rest of our flight and just about got laughed out of the airport. They had one empty seat to D.C. the following Tuesday, and we could flip for it, but if we didn't want to take a chance on waiting they'd put us up for the night at a hotel, then we could go to the railroad station next morning and work our way east by train, and that's exactly what we did. We stood in line for what seemed like hours and finally got two uppers for Kansas City. Once there, we stood in line again and got two uppers for Chicago. Once there, we stood in line again and got two uppers for Washington where we arrived on Saturday morning. I spent Saturday and Sunday with my father and aunt, and took the Federal Express for Springfield Sunday night, which got me in Monday morning. Got to East Longmeadow to find Miss Ellis had had to leave the day before for another baby case, and Sis and daughter Babs had moved in.

It seems Russ had been having an affair, for which I never really blamed him. Sis and his parents all treated him like a juvenile delinquent; he even had to ask Sis for 15 cents to buy cigarettes. I never could figure out why Sis didn't move in with her own family who lived in nearby Forest Park and had plenty of room, rather than crowding in with Bob's family in East Longmeadow. However, as you'll see it turned out to be a good thing for me that she did. They sent Russ to Wyoming to stay with Uncle Al, like a bad little boy put in the closet for punishment.

I spent the day getting reacquainted with Anne, who had thrived under Miss Ellis's expert care. I was quite worn out, so didn't hurry to pack up Anne and Willie and return to Hingham, to our cozy but really lonesome little house. That same Monday evening the babies were in bed and the rest of us were relaxing in the living room when about 9 p.m. the phone rang. I answered and was completely astonished to hear the operator say: "I have a collect call from Lt. McCullough in Hartford—will you accept it?" I knew Bob was almost two weeks out in the Pacific and thought someone was playing games, but said "yes"—and then it really was Bob on the phone. A couple of pilots had been killed, and the ship had returned to San Diego with the bodies. While the ship was in port (only overnight) orders came through for Bob to report in to Radar School in Norfolk. The skipper wasn't happy about losing Bob, who thought he'd find some way to have his order rescinded. So as soon as Bob was released, he packed up his gear and headed for the airport; didn't even stop to cash a check and had the magnificent sum of $1.00 on him. The airlines took a check for his ticket but wouldn't cash one, so he came across the country on a dollar. By the time he got to Brainard Field all he had left was a dime to call the operator. Imagine—I'd left San Diego on a Tuesday and finally struggled into Springfield the following Monday, whereas Bob had left on Sunday and arrived the next day. Being in uniform did have some advantages. He had a few days' leave before he had to report in, and we were in a quandary as to what to do. We didn't know how long he'd be in Norfolk but presumed at least six months, and I wanted to be with him. Finally we decided to give up the house, take Anne and Willie and go to Norfolk. Bob's parents were horrified at the thought of our taking a 3-month old baby into conditions about which we knew nothing, and they were right, but I was determined to be with Bob, so they offered to keep Anne until I could find a place to live down there. We thought it would be for perhaps two weeks, but it turned out to be two long months before we would see her again.

We took a hurried trip to Hingham, got rid of the house (not without pangs; we had such beautiful months there) put all our furniture in storage except my sterling silver flatware. I can't imagine why I wanted to keep it with me; it presented a problem throughout the rest of the war. Perhaps subconsciously I wanted some tangible evidence of our life together as it had been before the world fell apart.

On a rainy morning in early December Bob, Willie, I and the sterling silver took off for Norfolk. It was a long hard drive, no turnpikes or super highways, just macadam roads that meandered through every town. When we pulled into Norfolk about 6 p.m. it was dark with a wet snow falling, and we had no place to go. Every motel, hotel, boarding house, even brothels were full up. Even the chaplain on the base had no suggestions for us. Bob could have stayed at B.O.Q. with no difficulty, but he had his wife and dog on his hands.

I don't know how he happened to think of it, but he suddenly remembered an address that one of the pilots on the Bogue had given him when he heard that Bob had been transferred to Norfolk: a rooming house in Ocean View, halfway between Norfolk and Virginia Beach. It was owned by the Yates who had sons in the Navy and were said to be sympathetic toward Navy couples. We drove there and I sat in the car hardly daring to hope, but soon Bob came out to say they had a room we could have for the night, but we'd have to leave in the morning as it was rented to a couple who were expected the next day. They weren't too enthusiastic about Willie as Mr. Yates didn't like dogs. This amused us in thinking back because before we left Willie and Mr. Yates were such good friends that the former spent many hours cozily ensconced on the latter's lap.

The bed could have been full of rocks that night and we wouldn't have noticed. A warm room and a roof over our heads were more than we had expected, and even better, next morning Mrs. Yates said we could have the room for a few more days as the expected couple had been delayed. So Bob went off to the

Air Station to report in. I can never remember what I did all day long in all those places to pass the time until evening, when Bob and I could be together. At least I had lots of company; all us wives were in the same boat, savoring each moment we had with our husbands, never knowing how long they would last, or if they would ever come again. Several days later Mrs. Yates told us she had an attic room we could have for the rest of our stay. We were delighted. There was no heat, but she lent us an electric heater, and there were plenty of covers. The best thing about it was that we had our own bathroom; the three couples on the second floor had to share one. We had no shower or tub, but Bob took his showers at the Station and I became an expert at taking a bath in the basin, now and then finding time to luxuriate in the tub downstairs when it was unused. The population of Norfolk had expanded so that the water pressure at certain times was practically nil, and it took a couple of hours to get enough water in the tub for a decent bath.

One difficulty was finding decent places to eat. There were plenty of restaurants but they were all lousy. They didn't have to be good with so many people wanting to eat they queued up in line and waited interminably for anything that was at least lukewarm, and didn't move when you tried to get it on your fork. Mrs. Yates evidently heard us complaining about this, and very kindly offered the use of the cellar if we wanted to cook communally. We jumped at the chance. It was primitive to say the least, but we had a lot of fun. We girls all went grocery shopping together and scrounged in all the grocery stores, and scrounging it really was. When the store got in a supply of canned tuna word got around, and the shelves would be bare in an hour, even with only one to a customer. Nobody realized what harm cigarettes could do so everyone smoked, but if you had a favorite brand, forget it. If you could buy two packs of a brand you'd never heard of you were fortunate, even though they tasted like burning rope.

Our kitchen facilities consisted of an old ice box, not electric, but it was winter and the cellar unheated so we didn't have to buy ice all that often. Our stove was a little two-burner gas stove, really a hot plate. We had a beaten up dish pan but no sink; we got hot water from an outlet in the water pipe that ran across the ceiling of the cellar. When we were through, somebody emptied the dish water out on the beach. Mrs. Yates lent us her cast-off utensils: pots and pans, unmatching plates and glasses, but we had my sterling silver which really dressed the cellar up. We took turns cooking, and crude as everything was I don't know when we'd had more fun. I can remember the name of only one couple, Bert and Anne Johnson. They were all ensigns attached to, I think, Little Creek. By then Bob had made J.G. so he outranked everyone. I wish I knew what happened to them all.

Chapter 6

Of course nobody could go home for Christmas, but Mrs. Yates invited us all to share Christmas dinner with her, which was most pleasant. We toasted everyone in grape juice as the Yates were teetotalers and would allow no spirits in their house. It was sad missing her first Christmas with Anne, but we knew she was being well cared for, and we had each other—so much more than many other people had.

As New Year's Eve approached we were all trying to decide how best to celebrate it. All the officer's clubs would be so crowded we decided the ideal place was the cellar. We tried to be terribly clever and take the liquor and ice in by the cellar door, so the Yates would never know we weren't spending a nonalcoholic evening. How naive can you be? It was a marvelous party and as midnight drew near we became more and more exuberant. Due to the fact that the husbands had to go to work tho next day we called a halt at 1 a.m. and started upstairs, reminding each other to tiptoe and be very silent so as not to wake the Yates on our way to bed. Somebody opened the cellar door and there were the Yates, waiting for us to file by one by one. As we did so sheepishly, we were told by a stone-faced Mrs. Yates that we were no longer welcome in her house and would have to be out by the end of the week. She wouldn't have such disgusting tipplers in her home. That surely put a damper on what had been a delightful, though I guess noisy party. The husbands sneaked off to work next morning, and we wives spent the day avoiding our landlady and wondering what we were going to do.

Bob came home that evening with word that he was to report in to the Belleau Wood which was under construction at the Philadelphia Navy Yard, which solved our housing problem in Norfolk, though we didn't know what we'd do in Philly, Willie being the problem. However, an enlisted man on the base told Bob of a hotel in Camden that took dogs. I never found out what happened to our good friends at Mrs. Yates's establishment, but she seemed to be thawing out somewhat, and hopefully they weren't kicked out as promised.

So we took our worldly goods, including Willie and my silver, and headed for Camden. We found the hotel right in the middle of the Camden business district, not very prepossessing to say the least. But the people were very nice and willing to take the dog, and we thought we'd only be there for a day or two so could put up with its flaws. However, we were there for three very long weeks. Bob was supposed to be detached from the Belleau Wood and sent to Floyd Bennett Field on Long Island. He was to be fighter director to the ship's two squadrons that were training there. The hitch was that his release had to be signed by some line officer who was really weird. He had an aversion to aviators to begin with, and further had a certificate on the wall which certified to his sanity. He kept Bob sitting around twiddling his thumbs for three weeks while I was going out of my mind with boredom.

Each day I would follow the same dull routine: got up and had breakfast with Bob. Walked the dog, went back to bed for a couple of hours for lack of anything else to do, walked the dog, did whatever laundry we had in the bath tub, read the newspaper from cover to cover, walked the dog. Listened to soap operas, simple, innocent little 15-minute sagas in those days—Ma Perkins, the Romance of Helen Trent, His Gal Sunday. Walked the dog. Didn't dare go to Philly or anywhere where I'd be gone more than an hour as I couldn't leave Willie alone too long.

After an eternity Bob would come home and we walked the dog, then went out for dinner and either to a movie or came home and played acey-deucy. At least we were together, which made up for everything else. A few days before we left we were wandering around looking for a place to eat, and came across a beautiful brand new hotel, the Walt Whitman. We went in to have dinner, and found out that they would take dogs—had kennels for them. Surely made our day to discover that instead of spending three weeks in that grubby little flea bag, we could have been wallowing in the lap of luxury. Oh well—maybe we'd have gone broke paying for it, and as I've said before, it really didn't matter where we were as long as we were together.

At long last the officer condescended to sign Bob's release, so we took the dog, the silver, and the rest of our worldly goods and headed for Long Island. Rockaway was the nearest city to Floyd Bennett, so we headed directly there. We arrived about 4 p.m. and went directly to a real estate office. The lady said it was too late to see places that afternoon, so she directed us to a nearby hotel and said she'd pick us up first thing in the morning.

Rockaway and Far Rockaway (where we ended up) were summer towns and quite deserted in February. The hotel was closed for the season but had a few rooms open for people like us. When we saw it our hearts plummeted; another flea bag, but this looked as if it were made of construction paper held together by Tinker toys—remember them? There was a huge, very aggressive police dog in the lobby, and we had a terrible time getting Willie by him. The room hadn't been cleaned since the previous summer and when I went to take a bath, water just trickled out of the faucet leaving little rivulets of white in the grimy tub. The room next door was occupied and the walls so thin they might as well not have been there. It's occupant coughed and snored all night, and it almost seemed he was in the same bed with us. But we were tired and (the old refrain) we were together, and we slept all night waking to a beautiful

71

morning of what proved to be a beautiful day. The real estate agent came around at 9 a.m. and we had no difficulty finding a satisfactory little house. It was supposedly built of packing crates left over from World War I planes, but it seemed sturdy, though the floors all slanted in different directions. It had a dirt cellar with a voracious oil burner which kept us nice and warm, but it kept eating up our oil allotment. Poor Bob was forever running to the local ration board which couldn't have been kinder; nothing was too good for service people. We found that to be true of all the tradespeople, a very refreshing difference from the way we had been treated in Norfolk.

As Far Rockaway was a summer community at that time, we were the only people on the block except for a very interesting Navy couple, Baker by name, across the street. They came from a small town in Florida (population 400) and had never been anywhere until he went to a nearby college and became a 90-day wonder. It was enjoyable taking them in to New York; the simplest things that we took for granted in a large city amazed them. They had a baby girl the same age as Anne whose name was Bonnie; I remember it because there was a popular singer at that time named Wee Bonnie Baker.

We went to East Longmeadow to pick up Anne, and it was the first time that Bob, Anne, and I and Willie, too, had lived together as a family except for the two days' emergency leave in Hingham, and we really enjoyed it. The same old sword of Damocles still hung over our heads (i.e. his departure at any moment for the Pacific war zone) but aside from that we had a lovely normal life for the next three months. There were disadvantages, such as no washing machine (no laundromats or disposable diapers then) so I spent a lot of time washing Anne's large laundry. When the weather was bad there was no place to hang it except around the kitchen or on radiators. They didn't dry soft and fluffy, so poor Anne had the worst case of diaper rash of any small dependent in the U.S. Navy.

We became very expert at finding our way by subway into New York. We saw quite a few shows, and the Ringling Bros. Circus when it opened at Madison Square Garden. Somebody in the squadron had a dinner party almost every weekend. One Saturday night the squadron had a dinner party at some elegant hotel in the city (can't remember which). It was a long subway trip into town and a lengthy and freeflowing cocktail hour, and it wasn't until I was seated at the dinner table that I realized I desperately needed the ladies' room and had no idea as to its whereabouts. Since Bob was one of the senior officers we were seated at the head table directly across and as far as possible from the door to the hall which led, no doubt, to my desired destination. I asked Bob in a whisper if he knew where the restrooms were. Instead of answering me he stood up, tapped on his glass, and when the room quieted, announced, "My wife has to go to the bathroom. Does anyone know where it is?" Today that would have bothered me not a whit, but 45 years ago I still retained traces of my ante-bellum super modesty so I got up and started with red face for the door. Surprisingly, about three-fourths of the wives got up and trooped out with me, all of us in the same state but no one with the nerve to instigate a hejira. The incident broke the ice, and the rest of the evening was most relaxed and enjoyable—even the long ride home on the subway in the early morning hours. As with all good things, it had to come to an end. Bob came home one night in mid-April and said the squadrons had been ordered aboard ship, and he was going with it on its shake-down cruise. So he left for Philly, and Anne, Willie, the silver and I went in the opposite direction, back to East Longmeadow to stay with Bob's mother and dad.

I wasn't exactly exuberant about it. Sis and Babs and their dog Bubbles were still there. Russ was in Wyoming trying to get himself together working on Uncle Al's ranch, and didn't seem anxious to come back, though family pressure forced him into it the following fall. By right of priority Sis had a large bedroom that ran the width of the house and Anne, Willie and I were crowded into a small sort of sewing room. It was okay for three of us, but when Bob came one weekend, after ferrying a plane from Philly to Pratt & Whitney and wangling an overnight leave, it was a crowded little room, especially with a three-quarter size bed. Sis didn't offer to change with us so there we were, but it really was 100% nicer with four of us than with just three.

Bob said he hoped to get a weekend leave and, if I could come to Philly we could stay with the Masters; Al was attached to another carrier, same class as the Belleau Wood, being built at the same time and place; and they had rented a pretty little farmhouse outside of Camden. One day in mid-May Bob called and I made plans to go, but as I didn't have a train schedule I said it would be sometime in the afternoon, and I'd send a telegram with time of arrival c/o our indispensable go-between, Commandant of the Naval District.

Everything would have gone without a hitch if it hadn't been for Betty Masters, a most devoted friend of whom I was very fond. However, she was really fey to the nth degree, and if there was any way to foul up a simple situation she'd find it. My telegram said I'd be arriving in Philadelphia at 2:30 p.m. To me there was no other station in Philly but 30th St. which was also Penn Station and the main one. But Betty said I could be getting off at North Philadelphia or even Broad St. station, and thereby reduced Bob to a state of utter confusion.

He was at 30th St. Station when I got in, but in all the crowds we missed each other at the train gate, and there ensued four hours of Keystone cops around the station, in and out of doors, never coming face to face. We each had the other paged but neither paid attention thinking it was our own page. During the afternoon Bob also went to North Philly and to Broad St., of course with no luck. If anyone thinks we were utterly stupid, let me explain that during the war railroad stations and airports were at most times wall-to-wall people, half servicemen and half civilians greeting them or saying goodbye, and finding someone in that mass of humanity wasn't easy. Finally around 5 I called Betty, who was at an aunt's in Ithan, a nearby suburb. She hadn't heard from Bob and said I might as well come out there so I headed for the ticket window, and there discovered I no longer had a pocketbook. I tore back to the phone booth in panic, and there it was on the floor where I'd left it while dialing—wouldn't have been there two minutes had it been the present day. So off I went, and just as I arrived the phone rang—Bob with the same hope that he might reach me through Betty. His first words were "Where in hell have you been?"

Chapter 7

Betty, Al, and I drove back to Philly and met Bob at the Benjamin Franklin. We were so tired of running that they left us there and went on to Camden. The only available space was the bridal suite, and we took it thankfully, happy as any bride and groom. Next day we went to the Masters' and spent the weekend at their home. Al and Bob were going to sea again for about a month, but then the carriers would be in the Philly Navy Yard for six weeks, getting fitted out to leave for the Pacific war zone. Betty and Al asked if I wouldn't like to bring Anne and Willie and stay with them until the boys left. It sounded like heaven to me—much easier saying goodbye to Bob and taking a crowded train back to Springfield, knowing I'd seen him again shortly, and we could spend some time together. It would also be easier than living with Bob's parents and their dog, plus Sis and Babs and their dog—all in a house that wasn't and never would be mine. Keeping house has always been at the bottom of my list, coming as I did from a southern environment where there was inexpensive domestic help. They were all black and all people of whom I was very fond, like members of the family. Bob's mother greatest pleasure was in all types of cleaning, cooking, laundry, etc., and she and Sis took it for granted that it was everyone else's heart's delight too. However, we did manage to get along fairly well, and when things got to be a little more than I could stand, I'd take Willie and Anne and walk down through the meadows that stretched for a mile or so in back of the house—no people, just pretty little birds, flowers, trees, and sometimes a rabbit.

Bob called in mid-June and said to come on down, so once again I loaded up the car with all Anne's paraphernalia, Anne, Willie, the silver, and an added attraction which I took along from then on: a metal cruise box in which I stored items that were hard to get even when you traded at a grocery store regularly but impossible in a strange town: canned roast beef, canned ham, tuna fish, pineapple juice—the list of rationed items was endless. I also took Bob's mother, who was going on to Baltimore to visit friends. It did make it easier to have her along to help with Anne, who was at a very wiggly age. It took nearly all day to get there, but it wasn't a bad trip, and of course it was so good to be with Bob again.

This proved to be another nice interim for Bob and me. We were very compatible with the Masters, and time slipped by much too fast. One day I cleaned out Betty's refrigerator while she was in Philly for the day. Though housekeeping was very boring to me, if things got too dirty I suddenly couldn't stand it and had to shovel out. Betty was completely indifferent to dust and dirt, so every time she'd go off I'd complete a project, mostly because I was concerned about Anne's survival. The refrigerator was a disaster area, full of little bowls of this and that which Betty thought she'd use but never did. In a far corner of the lowest shelf sat a bowl of spaghetti I had made the weekend we visited two and a half months ago, a touch on the green side.

Betty and I spent one afternoon chasing a small pig. We heard the dogs, Willie and her Ricky, barking furiously down by a pond on the edge of their property. When we investigated, we found them in pursuit of a pig, about 4 months old. We put the dogs in the house and took up the pursuit ourselves, and I've never spent another such hysterical 45 minutes. This was the most elusive pig I'd ever seen; every time we thought we had him cornered he'd run between our legs. I didn't have enough nerve, but Betty would grab him by a leg or an ear, then he'd slip away from her. Finally, we backed him up between the barn and fence and forced him inside. We had visions of roast pig with apple in mouth, for once having enough meat to be lavish with. Unfortunately, our consciences got the better of us—and we couldn't have eaten him anyhow after having been so intimately acquainted. Betty called the state police and a very relieved farmer came to pick him up—seems he'd fallen off the truck on the main highway.

In Mid-August Bob came home one night and said not to expect him home anymore so the next night we all went out to dinner, then drove him to the dock. He had to be aboard by 1900 hours. A few weeks later we did the same for Al. There was no point in our hanging around as we knew they were both headed for the Pacific war zone. Betty decided to go back to her family's home in San Diego, and I decided to go to Washington and stay with Wo for a while. She and Tom had bought a house in Bethesda, Maryland, and he also was out in the Pacific.

10 Sept.
At sea

My darling,

Haven't been writing since we left 24 August. I couldn't send them and couldn't write much news, anyway, but think I see a chance to get this off by a flight, and it may be a good long time before we get back to port. Don't worry about long intervals as we expect to be in and out for the rest of our stay.

Good hunting so far. Been out across the equator and 180 degree meridian and just aching to get back to P.H. and a good glass of beer. Feeling pretty good and everything okay. My gang doing really well. Have had our share of contacts and so far lead the field.

"BEWARE, ALL POLLYWOGS," SAID THE GHOSTLY VOICE OVER THE BLATT BOX

To say that the Belleau Wood had crossed the equator several times during the preceding days is a simple statement of little import. But to the men aboard who had never before seen that glorious line, the crossing had reverberating significance. These greasy, slimy, "pollywogs" were now eligible for initiation into the elite order of shellbacks. (A "pollywog" is any person who has never crossed the equator; a "shellback" has.)

Here's Don W. Shearson, PhoM1c with his account of "from pollywog to shellback":

"Tales of terror trickled throughout the ship, horrible accounts of the process of being converted from a slimy pollywog to a nice, clean shellback; but the sudden warning via the announcing system was the tipoff of what was to follow.

That was shortly after a routine G.Q. one evening. The following morning found pollywogs dressed in backward togs—everything but their shoes worn hindside to and inside out. Some were dressed in outfits that included everything from funnels to lengths of fire hose; other sprouted bright-colored pajamas. Pollywog lookouts spent all morning on the forward end of the flight deck, peering through the wrong end of telescopes, waiting to see the 'line' as we approached it. In accordance with the backward trend, they were of course looking toward the fantail.

Eventually each pollywog received a summons to the court of Neptunus Rex, the summons stating the offense for which he was to be tried. And the charges were in keeping with all that had gone on before; they ranged from impersonating a shellback to attempting to steal the royal baby's nipple.

Finally the notorious day arrived. The morning was one of torture. At noon the victims were stripped down to their shorts and herded onto the hangar deck. In groups of 50 they were escorted by sentries to the flight deck; well packed canvas tubes made good persuaders and discouraged mutiny.

Arriving upon the flight deck, each pollywog was forced to his knees, encouraged by electric pitch forks. Traveling across the flight deck on hands and knees, the victim was paraded before the Royal Party, including the Royal Baby, whose navel had to be kissed. Generously smeared with a vile-tasting concoction, the extremely fat *baby's paunch wasn't an inviting place, especially when one's head was pushed from behind. ('Royal Baby' usually was the most corpulent shellback aboard).*

After the parade, things began to get hot. Tall men were forced into a wooden coffin several inches to short, then made to lie down in it, scooting back and forth as a club was pounded from one end to the other. If you didn't scoot fast enough—well!

A wild eyes 'doctor' had his operating table all rigged up, including electric saws and wicked-looking mallets. Another 'doctor' snapped, "Say ahhhhhh', then jammed a paint brush with more of the vile vitamins, down the pollywog's throat. Busy barbers made bad haircuts worse.

The stocks were reserved for special cases of stubborn recalcitrants who were locked in, battered with salt water from a hose, painted with more of the royal baby's belly cosmetics, grease, oil, rotten eggs—and just pestered in general.

Came the climax of the entire initiation: running the sleeve. A couple of target sleeves had been sewn together end to end making a three-foot tunnel almost 40 feet long through which each candidate was forced to crawl with a fire hose stream of salt water driving through from behind. The biggest shellbacks with more of those canvas persuaders flanked the tunnel. Nuff said. It was either keep your head down and the other end up—or be carried to sick bay for reviving.

All of this process produced new shellbacks, with the predominant color for a few days in the blacker and bluer hues. Other than the bruises, each victim had one thing to show for the ordeal; an impressive certificate signed by the skipper saying the bearer had been 'duly initiated into the order of shellbacks.' "[1]

# # #

My darling,

The army flew in some mail for us, and I was so happy to hear from you after such a long time. Hadn't had a thing since 3 August and was sure worried. Anyway, know now you are in Washington all safe and sound. Sounds like it must be quite a panic there, but I guess you girls like it.

Miss you more than ever and miss my little daughter. Grew to love her very much and want so badly to be around to watch her grow up. Guess lots of kids are growing up without any men around. Wonder what effect it will have on them. Anne probably won't have anything to

78

do with me if I stay away much longer.
    This is hurried, but I did want to get it off to you if I
could.

                    I love you,
                    Bob

                    # # #

It seemed like a perfect solution; Wo and I had always gotten
along so well; we'd be company for each other, as would Mark,
Pattie, and Anne. And I really couldn't face another winter with
Bob's family. Sis was still there, and if I couldn't be with Bob I
at least wanted to live in my own life style. So I packed up the
dog, the baby, the silver and the cruise box, and Betty and I
drove to Washington. Betty planned to visit us for a week, then
pick up her car and dog and head for California. Wo was visiting
in Norfolk, but Mattie Mae and the children were there so we
settled in comfortably. It was nice to be back with my own
family and I was looking forward to, if not a happy time, at least
a relaxing one with my sister to whom I'd always been so close.
    Sadly, when she came home we found we didn't agree on
anything. I think there were two reasons: one, we were
completely at odds on child rearing, and two, though I didn't
know it then, Tom's infidelity was beginning to show. He should
have lived in a polygamous society, and Wo, I think,
subconsciously, resented the good relationship Bob and I had. It
was her house, though I paid my share, and as long as things
were done her way we managed to get along. In our compatible
moments we had some very enjoyable times. We both found the
hardest time of day between 4 and 6 p.m. when we'd see all the
husbands coming home. We resented them bitterly, especially our
next-door neighbor, an R.A.F. officer enjoying life in
Washington while our husbands were out in the Pacific. They
sometimes got ashore for R & R, but it was usually a remote
place like Ulithe, a small Pacific island. Bob said the rain and
wild pigs ran under their cots at night, and he picked up malaria
which plagued him for years afterward. Wo and I often had a pre-
dinner drink, but we didn't think it ladylike for two females to
sit around drinking martinis or old-fashioneds so we slowly
sipped sherry—much more potent, actually than a mixed drink.

                    10 October, Sunday
                    At sea—(Baker & Tarawa)[2]

My darling,
    Getting back in tomorrow. Been a pretty exciting trip
and be glad to sit around for awhile.
    Haven't written any letters knowing they wouldn't

79

Anne's first steps, Fall of 1943—watched over by Willie.

Mark, Pattie and Anne, Washington, D.C., Winter of '44.

get off. *The worst of leaving is going without hearing from you.*

Spent our anniversary in the very middle of all the doings but hope my letter reached you. Seems like a million years since I wrote you last. These trips seem to last that long, and I get all mixed up in times and dates.

There is nothing I can say about our trip except that things went well with me and my boys stole the show again. I'm fine and dandy but blue and lonesome for you.

> *I love you*
> *Bob*

7 December
(Mayen & Kwajalein)

My darling,

How are my darling wife and little girl? It has been so long, and I think of you with every breath. Hope my three letters did get off to you. Been out quite a spell and wanted you to know everything was OK. We're on our way in but just for a short while.

Had a tough time and sure glad to have it over with for a while. No tea party and figure we had several horseshoes planted on us somewhere. Many of the others weren't so lucky, but all in all we sure gave the stinkers a good beating they won't soon forget.

Just a year ago today I got my new orders and was on my way home to you and Radar school in Norfolk. I wonder if I could have another set waiting for me now in P.H.

> *Loving you and having you love me is all the happiness I ever need.*
> *Bob*

25 December

Oh, my darling,

Sit down and don't get too excited for here is your, Anne's and my Christmas present.

"When relieved, detached from U.S.S. Belleau Wood. Proceed first available government transportation (air) to nearest U.S. port. Proceed and report to Cdr Air Station, Norfolk for temporary duty for further orders to C.O. of fighting squadron. 15 days leave."

Don't know when I'll be relieved. It may be a month or so, but, anyhow, darling will be home to you very soon.

Haven't opened my Christmas presents yet but will right now.

Still pretty dizzy from the good news and a hell of a

*hangover from a Christmas party last night. Guerrieri who
is C.O. of a fighter squadron here and Al were with me
and the three of us had a swell time. Guerry stayed aboard
with me and just left for his base.*

*Golly, I love you, my darling and will be home in your
arms soon.*

Bob

*p.s. Please call folks. Have only one stamp and may be
several days before I get around to writing them.*

27 December

My dearest wife,

*I can hardly make sense these days—honestly don't
know up from down or black from white. It's all so
unbelievable and so good.*

*Funny, I know you haven't yet received the first letter
about my orders. It will probably catch up to you about
New Year's Day.*

*The hardest thing is to wait for my relief. It may be a
month or longer, and I hate to think of going back out
next time because it is going to be a long one.*

*Finished packing today and going to ship it right
away so I'll get a head start.*

*When I do get relieved I should be able to leave pretty
much in a hurry. Have Clipper transportation, I expect,
and hope I can get airline reservations across country.*

*We are getting all set for the fireworks. Hate to think
of bucking Norfolk again, but maybe it will be better
under orders to the squadron. It will probably be away
from Norfolk in the beginning anyway.*

I love you,

Time went by, Thanksgiving, then Christmas. It seemed as
though one or another of the children had a cold all winter. We
had a marvelous concoction for coughs handed down for
generations, no doubt by my spirits loving ancestors, which we
kept on the bathroom shelf. It consisted of equal parts of
bourbon, honey, glycerin, lemon juice and water. Years later
when I first had asthma and didn't know it I went through a
period of waking up at 2 a.m. each morning coughing and
gasping. I would drag myself down to the kitchen and mix the
above in an old-fashioned glass and sip it until the coughing
slowly but surely subsided. Of course, Bob teased me about
faking the cough so I could have the drink.

One afternoon the children were all hacking away so we gave
them each a tablespoon of the above-mentioned elixir and put
them for their naps. Anne and Mark woke up bright-eyed and

bushy-tailed, but Pattie slept peacefully on and nothing we did could rouse her. We were close to pushing the panic button when someone noticed the empty cough medicine bottle under the bathroom sink. Pattie had evidently gotten up and swigged down the whole bottleful. She finally woke up around dinner, subdued but with no evident hangover. Needless to say we found a new and more inaccessible home for the bottle.

Russ and Sis reconciled and were living in Silver Spring. The Fergusons were at Patuxent, and I left Anne with Wo and had such a nice weekend with them there (My close friend and roommate Betty Harris had married John Ferguson in December 1939, also in Coronado) at the time when the Navy was involved at Truk. While officially I didn't know that Bob and the Belleau Wood were there, actually I did, and it was somehow reassuring to be with Betty and John.

14 January
(Tarda & Kwajalein)

Dearest Anne,

Feeling rather blue tonight—going away instead of on my way home to you as I thought I might be. We go out Sunday so this is my last chance to write to you for many days. Maybe even be home before any more letters reach you. I figure as close as I can around the first of March.

Going to be the biggest thing yet and suppose I ought to be happy to be in on it, only, honey, I want to see you and be with you more than anything else.

Captain Pride had me down today for a talk and said he was happy my relief didn't show up and not to feel too badly as he wouldn't have let me go, anyway. I hope I can justify his belief in me and do a good job. It will be nice some day to sit by the fire and tell you all about it.

Had a couple of beer dates with Al the past few days. He is OK but hasn't heard much from Betty.

By the way if Betty and Fergie are still about tell them that Uncle Mark (Admiral Mischer was Betty's uncle) is in charge of the works.

Will give you a call from Frisco if I ever get there so don't be looking for me in every corner.

Everything is going to be okay, and I'll be back in your arms before you can say Jack Robinson.

I'll be thinking of you and loving
you with every beat of my heart.

# # #

In March 1944 Bob was due to arrive on leave, and my aunt, who had lived in Washington for many years, insisted I get a new, jazzy outfit in which to welcome him. She helped me pick out a very good-looking suit, black skirt with black and white houndstooth jacket and top coat (the latter I still had 40 years later, though it ended up as a garden coat at the lake). Also I got black patent Mary Janes, a large, bright red cartwheel hat and matching purse. I'd surely be the grandest tiger in the jungle.

Then began our usual changes, delays and related phone calls. Bob called Saturday evening from Chicago and said the airport was fogged in, and he was taking a train due to arrive in Washington at seven the following morning. So I laid out all my gorgeous clothing and went to bed, waking early in the morning to the rattle of sleet—the weather front had moved from Chicago to D.C. It was about 45 minutes from Wo's house to the station, and I was petrified of driving the icy streets, but would have gone to meet Bob if I'd had to walk barefoot. Didn't wear my beautiful clothes, but instead my old Harris tweed coat, brown Knox hat and loafers—and miracle of miracles, the train was on time, and Bob was on it. Typical of Washington weather by noon the sun was out, sleet and snow melted away and it was like an early spring day. Anne hadn't heard a male voice in some five or six months, and at first every time Bob spoke, she cried. However, she soon grew used to it, aided by his taking her for her first ice cream cone—quelle mess!

We were so busy all day that I completely forgot my new outfit, but suddenly remembered as we were getting ready for bed that night. Clad in my most luxurious nightie I went to the closet, and came out with my new red hat on. The combination was so ludicrous, and Bob laughed so hard that I never afterward wore the hat, but carried it everywhere with me along with the silver and metal cruise box. It ended up about ten years later as a dress-up hat for Anne and friends.

When I heard Bob was coming home, my sister and Mattie Mae kindly offered to keep Anne and Willie so that Bob and I could have a week by ourselves. I'd found several places nearby, but when I told Bob, he said we couldn't possibly go anywhere but to East Longmeadow, as his family would be terribly hurt if we didn't visit them. The comparison between spending a week all by ourselves and spending it with his family, where Bob and Anne and I slept in one room, and I spent so much time caring for Anne, was odious to say the least. But as I've said before, being with him under any circumstances was so much better than being without him that I didn't argue much, and we spent his precious seven-day leave with his family.

Bob had to report in at Norfolk, so we drove back to D.C. and he left Anne and me at Wo's. Discovered with apprehension that Wo was in the hospital with scarlet fever. She was due to be released in a few days, and Tom was due home from the Pacific in a day or two. I felt completely in the way and didn't know

84

where to turn. Finally after some wangling and pulling of strings by Bill McCormick, an old friend from Coronado days, I got through to Bob in Norfolk. He had his orders to Charlestown, R.I., as skipper of an experimental night fighter squadron. This was VFN-90 (originally VFN-103), and the original for its logo "The Bat Lady", which was drawn by Milt Canniff, now hangs in the Yorktown Museum near Charleston, S.C. Bob said for me to go back to East Longmeadow and wait for him there. So I called Bob's mother and to my consternation she said she didn't want me; she'd just taken the crib down and cleaned the house and didn't feel up to it, a double blow since I hadn't wanted to go there in the first place. I called Bob again and he said I was to go anyway. Russ said the same thing, and they must have put pressure on their dad because he called that night and said Bob's mother had misunderstood—she thought I wanted to come back to stay for good, and for me to please come. I did so with a great deal of trepidation and not much elation.

[1]Excerpt from "Flight Quarters"—the war story of the U.S.S. Belleau Wood.

[2]The place names in parentheses at the beginnings of Bob's letters were not, of course, originally there due to censorship. I have, after research, added them for clarification.

Chapter 8

Bob showed up a couple of days later, reported in at Charlestown and in only a few days had found us a delightful house in Wakefield, Rhode Island, a large ranch type with a huge boulder for foundation and a cellar hewn out of that. It was just off the Boston Post Road and a little hill separated it from the road so we couldn't see it. Nobody knew a house was there, on a salt pond and facing out over Narragansett Bay.

We found we had an intriguing landlady, Mrs. Peterson, by name. She must have been in her eighties but was a chipper little person—with her white hair styled in a Dutch bob and forever topped by a black velvet beret which made her look like a super-annuated Buster Brown. She had white, white dentures that clicked merrily away when she talked. Bob said he saw her quite often along the road carrying a large carpetbag and thumbing frantically for a ride. Every once in a while she would turn up on our doorstep with the carpetbag bulging mysteriously and asking to go down to the cellar. There was a large locked room down there into which she would go, carefully locking the door behind her. There would be rummaging sounds for a few minutes. Then she would emerge and with carpetbag deflated take her leave.

Bob's curiosity finally got the better of him. There was no way you could see inside the room from the cellar, but there was a large window high up on the outside wall. He somehow rigged up a ladder and climbed up to peer through the window. He said the sight was indescribable. Articles piled on every available surface—silverware of every description, crystal bowls and vases, lamps, toasters—anything that would fit into the maw of her voracious carpetbag.

Our babysitter, Mrs. Browning, was the very nice wife of a nearby farmer, and she also boarded our landlady. We rather wondered if we would be considered the receivers of stolen goods so we asked Mrs. Browning what the scoop was. She said she had discovered that poor. Mrs. Peterson was light-fingered, and did what she could to retrieve the articles she found in Mrs. Peterson's room. She had no idea there was such a treasure trove in our rented house. Another mystery of our war travels of which we never knew the outcome.

By this time Bob had made Lieutenant Commander, and for the next year due to some strange quirk of euphony was called more often than not Lt. McCander McCullough instead of by his proper designation. When I stop to think about it, I really didn't know much about the serious aspects of Bob's 12 years as a Navy pilot. He was in the Pacific war theatre on two different tours of duty: six months, from August 1943 to February 1944 as Fighter Director Officer aboard the Belleau Wood, and for ten months as skipper of the Navy's first night fighter squadron attached to the Enterprise from August 1944 to June 1945. All I know of those tours I read in a couple of books in which he is mentioned, and in the Log of VF(N)90 a copy of which he brought home. I discovered he had received three Air Medals and several commendations though he poo-pooed the former and said everybody had them. I also found he was part of just about every battle and raid that took place in that area, including flying over Tokyo, Korea, and the coast of China. In all that time he was wounded only once, by the Enterprise's elevator which was used to lower aircraft from the flight deck and vice versa. Someone forgot to tell him it was being lowered and he walked right out into space. Fortunately he fell only about four feet and just got a cut on his leg. By the time he came home the scar wasn't even visible.

When Bob was at sea we wrote each other almost every day. His letters usually came through quite regularly, then suddenly they'd stop coming. I soon learned with trepidation that no mail meant some big operation was about to begin. There would be two or three weeks of rushing futilely to the door when the mailman came, and listening to news by commentators who actually knew less than I, as Bob was able to give me bits of information by innuendo. All mail was censored, but I knew he was on the Enterprise, and when he sent home his dress blues I realized he was about to go to the war zone. Once when there had been no mail for a couple of weeks I had a strange experience; it may sound silly, but it is true.

One night in early January of 1945 I became too restless to sit still. Anne was asleep so I took Willie for a walk in the meadows in back of the house. It was a clear, cold night with a full moon that was so bright I could see every detail of the terrain. Suddenly I felt so close to Bob, and all my restlessness disappeared; I went back home to bed and slept more peacefully than I had since Bob went away. Months later, while reading the squadron's log, I discovered that was the day Bob's plane went down in the ocean and he was listed as missing in action for 3 days. I don't think he'd have mentioned it if I hadn't discovered it in the aforementioned log.

It seems they sent the Navy in to soften up Manila so McArthur could emerge dramatically (and safely) from the sea to reclaim the city from the Japanese. There was a big plain in back of Manila with a mountain rising right in the middle of it. This was the route the planes took to get back to the carrier. Intelligence said the mountain had no guns so Bob didn't bother to avoid it, but Intelligence proved wrong, and as he flew by, anti-aircraft guns let go. They set his belly tank (which he was able to jettison) on fire and shot up his controls quite badly. Since radio silence was in effect he couldn't inform anyone of his plane's condition. He managed to tag along behind one of his squadron's planes back to the carrier, but when he attempted to land the controls were so unworkable that his plane went over the side and into the water, sinking almost at once. Bob was able to disentangle himself from his gear and was floating around in the Pacific when the U.S.S. Frank, (a destroyer sunk shortly afterwards by the Japs) picked him up. Due to radio silence and all the fighting going on they couldn't return Bob to the Enterprise, or even let them know he was safe. Hence his being listed as missing in action, for three days and also, thank Heaven, my not being informed of the fact.

On the night of March 9th of this year (1986) I was half watching a World War II documentary on television. The announcer remarked that it was a newly released one which had never been shown before so I started to pay closer attention, and when it switched from the European theatre to the Pacific and finally arrived at the retaking of Manila, I was glued to the set. The commentator said something to the effect that the fighting was almost entirely in the air and that, though it was an overwhelming victory for the U.S., a lot of the planes had not escaped unscathed. Suddenly on the screen appeared an aircraft carrier surrounded by puffs of anti-aircraft smoke and planes seemingly flying in all directions. The next five minutes was taken up with one shot after another of planes (both fighters and torpedo bombers) attempting to land on the carrier's flight deck. Some crashed into the island (super structure on the flight deck); some crashed into other planes standing there, but most went over the side and into the drink. I'm sure the facts could be proven one way or another, but I prefer to think that on this day I was a spectator to what had happened to Bob, and some forty-one years after it had happened, I saw him go overboard and disappear into the sea. Star Trek time warp or deja-vu?

Of course the good times were when Bob had shore duty, and the time he was at Charlestown was a period as close to perfection as possible under the circumstances. There were certain inconveniences but they were a challenge, and it was fun finding means to overcome them. The hot water heater burned wood, and I could never cope with it. Bob managed it nicely, but he'd be gone two or three days at a time and when the hot water ran out, I had to heat water on the stove, a bit tricky since my only receptacles were a large pail and a small teakettle. However, with some maneuvering on my part, we managed to stay reasonably clean. It was impossible to buy pots and pans as all metal went into the war effort. A phone was impossible to get, but since Bob was squadron commander, the telephone company provided one for us. However, we were on a ten-party line and at certain times of the day, forget it. Once in a while Bob would get off early at night, due to a fog that would sometimes drift in

Anne following in her Father's footsteps
—Charleston, R.I. Spring of 1944.

after sunset. I used to sit on our front porch overlooking the bay and watch for it to come in. Bob would try to call to tell me he was coming home, but seldom got through so he'd tell the switchboard operator to call me when she could. He usually got home before her call came through.

Later, due to our trust in our fellow man, we got into some difficulty over that telephone. When we moved out, another officer from the station moved in, and asked us to leave the phone connected until he could arrange to have it switched to his name. The first month I got a bill which was half ours and half his, so I sent the bill along with my check and asked him to take care of it. I got no more bills for a couple of months so assumed it had been changed to his name. Much later the phone company reached me in East Longmeadow with a bill for $50, quite a blow when in those days the normal phone bill was $6. Since the phone was still in our name we were responsible and had to pay. That first officer never bothered to have the name changed, and when he moved out, he left it for the next officer, etc. They made calls to Norfolk, Seattle, San Diego—fortunately for us there were no trans-ocean lines at that time.

There were many snakes around our place, little green ones that hung from trees and big black ones that lay across the path to the salt pond and deterred me from going down there unless Bob was with me. One day when Bob had been away for a few days I decided to go down in the cellar to see if I could coax the wood heater into burning. It was in a little back room up a couple of steps, and as the light was in the middle of the room I had to walk from daylight into dark. As I went up the steps I felt something flick between my legs. I turned on the light, and there was a large snake stretched across the steps. It showed no inclination to move, and I was so panicked I couldn't bring myself to step back over it but stood mesmerized with fear. At last my maternal instincts took over; Anne was alone upstairs. So I picked up the axe we used for kindling, chopped the snake into little pieces and fled up the stairs, closing the trap door in the living room. I had nightmares that night about the snake coming through the trap door and attacking Anne and me. It was a traumatic experience, though the snake was no doubt harmless, just looking for a cool place to snooze. Needless to say we lacked hot water until Bob returned.

We had a hard time getting meat and learned to make do with things we'd have turned our noses up at in ordinary times. Anne was fond of liver and we'd always had calves, but the only kind available was pork—just as good and even more nutritious. It was quite different from Far Rockaway, where merchants bent over backwards to help service families. Here they catered to their own, and we transients had to scavenge for ourselves. I found there were some tough old fowls around, so I'd buy them, boil them about half an hour in my galvanized bucket and then roast them. They were quite tasty. And our little salt pond yielded myriads of blue crabs. They were so stupid all we had to do was drop a piece of string with anything tied to it and they'd clamp on to the string. We pulled them out and dumped them into our indispensable bucket, which we later used to boil them. It was tricky getting the meat out of the shells, but they were so delicious it was well worth the effort.

We settled into a comfortable and happy routine. Bob went to work about 3 p.m. so I saved my domestic tasks until then, and often thought how silly I must have looked hanging out laundry as the sun went down. Anne and I would eat, and then I'd put her to bed and pass the evening as best I could. I'd go to bed at 11 and set the alarm for 1 a.m. so I'd be up when Bob got home to get him a snack before we went to bed to sleep as long as Anne would let us in the morning. A strange thing to remember: a whippoorwill lived somewhere on the hillside, and though his call was very melancholy it was somehow company; and I waited, with my constant companion, Willie, to hear him each night.

Chapter 9

Before we knew it May, June and July disappeared, and with August came Bob's orders to fly his squadron to the west coast, and from there they would go to Pearl Harbor to be attached to an unnamed carrier and thence to the Pacific War Zone. I couldn't stay where we were, so since Bob's parents had offered to let me stay with them again, we decided that was the best solution for the moment. We cleaned out the house and packed the car the night before as I didn't want to go back after Bob had left. Early next morning, Anne, Willie and I went to the air station to see him off, and watching the planes grow smaller and smaller and finally disappear was one of the hardest things to do. Since then I've never watched a plane, train or even an auto containing anyone I loved leave when it's for any length of time.

It was a hot August day as we three started our sad trip to East Longmeadow. The Chevy we'd bought in 1940 was a business coupe, with no back seat, just a high platform which made a marvelous play pen for Anne until this morning, when she learned to scramble over and fall into the front seat. She and Willie took turns going from back to front, and when she tired of that she began throwing out the window little extra things I had picked up to take along at the last minute: gloves, paperbacks, belts, etc. I was too hot and unhappy to stop for them. Since it was so hot, I'd opened the little wing windows (remember them?) to let as much breeze as possible blow in. Unfortunately we ran through a swarm of bees which also blew in, but luckily when I stopped the car, they blew right out again.

It took about two and a half hours from Charlestown to East Longmeadow, and at least it wasn't a boring trip. The first thing I did on arrival was to track tar onto Bob's mother's pale green wall-to-wall carpeting. It was so hot the new tar on their driveway had softened, and I would be the one to do the damage. Didn't help an already shaky relationship, though we did get along quite well on this tour of duty.

# # #

United States Pacific Fleet
U.S. Naval Air Forces
Fighting Squadron 103
10 August

Dearest Anne and little Anne,

Miss you both so very much. Sure was hard leaving you behind that day. Hope the zoom and the toilet paper shower were good and that everyone liked the show.

Our trip was without any troubles. Arrived on schedule,

and the boys behaved swell. *Going out to P.H. on CVE and expect about a month's further training here.*

Tried for two nights to call through but no luck. Lines all jammed, I guess.

Will write again on board and often. Have to load gear now.

> *Love you honey*
> *Bob*

14 August

My darling,

Just a note to say hi and that I miss you more than ever. Everything going smoothly and surely glad when I got the gang all rounded up and aboard C.K. Not doing much now but getting a good rest and lots of poker. Funny enough I'm ahead of the game. Have a tough job ahead, though and once started probably get no peace at all so making the best of it.

Trip across country went swell and thank God no trouble. Purcell had engine failure in New York, and we left Phil's group behind, but next day they caught up. Only made Atlanta the first night because of weather which made most of the rebels happy. Stayed in a jerk town, Midland, Texas the second night and arrived San Diego early Monday afternoon. Hard trip and plenty hot. Took about three days to get over my thirst.

Had a rip snorter of a party at the QC for the boys, band and all the works. Got dates at the Naval Hospital and all pippins. Took Betty Masters my self. She seemed to enjoy the gang and said they were in which is a lot for Betty to admit, right? We all went to the hotel Del afterwards. Several of the boys were plastered and raised hell, and I surely thought we would all end up in the jug.

> *Goodnight and sweet dreams,*
> *I love you*
> *Bob*

18 August

My darling sweet wife,

Bedtime and a chance to write. Had lots of time aboard but just too crowded and confused.

We are all settled here for a spell. Have wonderful quarters by my self—little screened in porch and all the fixings. Most of the gang three to a room. Swell station and will hate to leave it for a flat top. Have a jeep of my own—How do you like that? Starting operating in a day or so—mostly at night.

Lots of the VF 24 boys will soon be back out here.

Arky Snowden was killed at Truk also Stinky Ennis in the States. Joe Byros, too. Still and all most of the gang are still going strong and show up here sooner or later.

The stork has been busy in the squadron and think new arrivals total three or four—I've lost count. Mac had a girl, Young, a boy, Odom, a boy, and Latrobe a boy. Some others you don't know about. Rumor has it that Harry has trouble brewing back in R.I. Not sure about all the new boys but suspect that some of them ar expectant papas. The girl date situation has cleared up since a party we had, and now I'm faced with the other angle of everyone trying to get nights off. You can't win. They found some four hundred Wards at the Army center and seem to be quite content these days.

I'd fill the rest of the page with kisses but regulations won't allow it. Anyhow, here are a couple of hugs and kisses for you and little Annie.

> *Goodnight, sweet dreams, I love*
> *you*
> *Bob*

#

Had a letter from Betty Masters a few weeks later inviting me to come and stay with her at their house on Point Loma (San Diego). She was alone as Al was in the Pacific, too. It sounded like a perfect solution, but I felt I should check with Bob first; afterwards wished I hadn't. It took about three weeks to communicate, but when I got his answer he said he preferred to have me stay in East Longmeadow. It's hard to conceive now that I wouldn't have gone anyway, but I think any service wife would have agreed with me. We'd have posed naked as a statue in the park (no big deal nowadays) if it would have given our husbands any peace of mind. I remembered that Bob had spent a couple of nights in San Diego on his way out and had taken Betty to a couple of parties that had been such exuberant affairs I'm sure he'd didn't want me in that environment, and he was probably right. So I gave up and settled in to exist as best I could for however long it took till Bob was home again.

> *From Barbers Point—Honolulu*
> *VF(N) 90*
> *August 31*

My darling,

Golly here it is little Anne's birthday and she's two and a real big girl now. Things move so darn fast these days and our life has been so mixed up. Seems just like yesterday that we were riding in Tom's old car and had

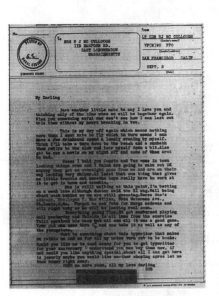

Letter 1 (Sept. 2)

To
MRS R J MC CULLOUGH
119 HAMPDEN RD.
EAST LONGMEADOW
MASSACHUSETTS

From
LT. CDR. R J MC CULLOUGH
VP(N)90 FPO
SAN FRANCISCO CALIF
SEPT. 2

My Darling

Just another little note to say I love you and thinking only of the time when we will be together again. Miss you something awful and don't see how I can last out this time without my heart breaking in two.

This is my day off again which means nothing more than I dont have to fly which in turn means I can have a few drinks and spend a lonely evening by myself. Think I'll take a turn down to the beach and a sunbath then retire to the club and tear myself down a bit. Also get to see a movie on my night off and none of them arnt so bad.

Guess I told you Jessie and Tex were in town looking things over and I think are going to make out OK anyway they are on their own from me and are on their way looking very chipper. At least that one thing that gives me little trouble and besides boys really have to work at it to get in here and trouble.

Mac is still waiting at this point, I'm betting on a week late although doctor said the Xt svg. Mail being about week behind so we are still guessing. Heres Sue's address, Mrs. Robert T. McMillan, 6026 Waterman Ave., St Louis, Mo. Forgot to ask Pete for Margs address and will right away so be will be leaving real soon.

Everything going fine.We got softball playing ball yesterday and thinking it will lame from the exercise. Paul smashed his back pad all and all it was a good game. They did one game there Q and one take it to as well as any of the youngsters.

We got a pounding about this typewriter that makes me rattle on and on for all my notes turn out to be books. Could you lik me to send money for you to get typewriter for your anniversary? A watercised you can buy them new, if I send would you like anything special, about all I can get here is jewelry maybe you would like another choping spree let me know honey right away.

Guess no more room, all my love darling
BOB

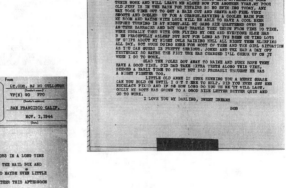

Letter 2 (Aug. 30, 1944)

To
MRS. R.J.MC CULLOUGH
119 HAMPDEN RD.
EAST LONGMEADOW
MASSACHUSETTS

From
LT. CDR. R.J. MCCULLOUGH
VP(N) 90
FPO SAN FRANCISCO
CALIFORNIA
AUG. 30, 1944

MY DARLING

JUST A NOTE TO SAY I LOVE YOU AND MISS YOU SO VERY MUCH.THINKING OF YOU ALL THE TIME HONEY AND JUST WAITING FOR THE DAY WHEN I CAN HOLD YOU IN MY ARMS AGAIN.

SUPPOSE THIS WILL TAKE LOTS LONGER THAN AIRMAIL BUT I IMAGINE ITS SEND GEE TO YOU SPENT SO OFTEN AND CONFUSION TOO. ID LIKE TO KNOW JUST HOW MUCH DIFFERENCE BETWEEN THEM AS THERE HAVE BEEN SEVERAL ARGUMENTS ABOUT IT.

FEELING BETTER TODAY THE SHOTS HAVE APPARENTLY DONE THEIR WORK AND WILL LEAVE ME ALONE NOW FOR ANOTHER YEAR.MY POOR OLD JEEP IS IN THE BARN FOR REPAIRS SO NO SWIM ING TODAY, ANY WAY TOOK TIME OUT TO GET A HAIR CUT AND SHAVE AND FEEL VERY SMOOTH AND COOLED UP FOR A CHANGE.HAVEING A COOLER RAINS FOR MY ROOM AND MAYBE WITH LUCK WILL BE ABLE TO HAVE A COOL BEER BEFORE TURNING IN AT NIGHT.ALL MY OARS ARE QUARTERED OVER IN ANOTHER BARRACKS AND BOY WHAT BRAWLS THEY THROW FROM TIME TO TIME. WERE USUALLY THRU WITH OUR FLYING BY ONE AND EVERYONE ELSE HAS B EN PEACEFULLY ASLEEP BUT NOT FOR LONG AS IVE BEEN OR TING LOTS OF GITTE ABOUT MY NIGHT OWLS RAIDING WELL ALL NIGHT THEN SLEEPING ALL DAY. NOT MUCH DOING HERE FOR MOST OF THEM AND THE GIRL SITUATION AS YOU CAN GUESS IS PRETTY SERIOUS. JONES AND TEX HAD A DAY OFF YESTERDAY SO MAYBE THE PICT URE HAS CHANGED I'LL CHECK UP ON IT WHEN I GO TO WORK.

GLAD THE FOLKS GOT AWAY TO MAINE AND SURE HOPE THEY HAVE A GOOD TIME. DID DAD TAKE EXTRA TEETH ALONG THIS TIME. SEEMED A EARLY TIME TO START BUT DAD PROBABLY THOUGHT HE WAS A NIGHT FIGHTER TOO.

LITTLE OLD ANNE IS SURE RUNNING YOU A MERRY CHASE CAN YOU HOLD ON UNTIL I G T T HER TO HELP. DID YOU EVER GET HER NECKLACE FIXED AND IF SO HOW LONG DO YOU TH NK IT WILL LAST. GOLLY MY NOTE HAS GROWN TO A GOOD SIZE LETTER BETTER QUIT AND GO TO WORK.

I LOVE YOU MY DARLING, SWEET DREAMS
BOB

Letter 3 (Nov. 1, 1944)

To
MRS. R.J.MC CULLOUGH
119 HAMPDEN RD.
EAST LONGMEADOW
MASSACHUSETTS

From
LT.CDR. RJ MC CULLOUGH
VP(N) 90 FPO
SAN FRANCISCO CALIF.
NOV. 1,1944

MY DARLING

HAVEN'T TRIED ONE OF THESE BIG JOBS IN A LONG TIME SO GUESS I'LL THROW ONE IN TO HELP FILL UP THE MAIL BOX AND KEEP YOU HAPPY. WILL TRY A DOUBLE SPACE AND MAYBE EVEN LITTLE ANNIE WILL BE ABLE TO READ IT. HAVE A BREATHER THIS AFTERNOON AND A PRETTY BUSY NIGHT COMMING UP AND PROBABLY WONT GET TO WRITE A REGULAR LETTER THIS EVENING.

NO NEWS AS USUAL EVERYTHING GOING WELL AND KEEPING AWFULL BUSY BUT SQUAD. IS SHAPING UP NICE AND GETTING ALOT OF GOOD EXPERIENCE. WITH ALL THE NEW BOYS IT KEEPS ME GOING TRYING TO REMEMBER THEM ALL BUT GUESS IN TIME IT WILL BE THE SAME AS THE OLD OUTFIT AND ALL ONE BIG FAMILY.

HARD TO THINK OF IT REAL FALLY BACK HOME AND IT MUST BE BEAUTIFUL, BET LITTLE ANNIE IS REAL CUTE AND WILL BE LOTS OF FUN THIS WINTER WITH THE SNOW ETC.,

I MISS YOU ALL SO AND THINK OF YOU WITH EVERY BEAT OF MY HEART HONEY,YOUR THE GRANDEST WIFE AND SWEETHEART IN ALL WORLD AND I LOVE YOU SO VERY MUCH.

ALL MY LOVE
BOB

To

MRS. R.J. MC CULLOUGH
IIO HAMPDEN RD.
EAST LONGMEADOW
MASSACHUSETTS

From

LT.CDR.RJ MC CULLOUGH
[Sender's name]'
VP(N) 90 FPO
[Sender's address]
SAN FRANCISCO, CALIF.

SEPT. I9,I944
[Date]

HELLO HONEY ME AGAIN

JUST THOUGH I'D THROW ONE OF THESE IN AGAIN
TO HELP FILL UP THE MAIL BOX AND THROW THE SCHEDULE
OFF SOME. YOU MAY HAVE TO USE A GLASS TO READ THIS
BUT GUESS YOU KNOW DARLING THAT I'M BETTING THAT YOU
COULD READ 1 love you STANDING ON YOUR HAED. ANY WAY
SWEETIE ALL MY LOVE IS YOURS AND I MISS YOU SO MUCH.
GOT A COUPLE OF HOPS THIS AFTERNOON AND A
LONG ONE TONIGHT BUT RIGHT NOW JUST PUTTERING AROUND
CLEANING UP ODDS AND ENDS. FINNALLY FINISH SOME OF
THE BUTTON WORK AND A FEW HOLES IN MY PANTS BUT I'LL
NEVER BE VERY GOOD AT IT I'M AFRAID.QUITE COOL AND
NICE HERE IN MY ROOM AND USUALLY NO ONE TROUBLES TO
COME WAY DOWN HERE FROM THE SQUAD TO BOTHER ME. HAVE
A PHONE BUT I NEVER TOLD ANYONE ABOUT IT SO IT NEVER
RINGS WHICH IS SWELL UNTIL THEY DISCOVER IT.
I SAW A SWELL BALL GAME YESTERDAY, THE NAVY
ALL STARS SPLIT UP AND PLAYED A EXIBITION GAME HERE.
ALL THE PLAYERS ARE MAJOR LEAGUE STARS AND IT WAS A
REAL TREAT. SCHOOLBOY ROE,DICKEY,DI MAG, SEARS, RIZZUTO
BRANCATO,GORDEN,PRIDDY AND LOTS OF OTHERS. THE ARMY
HAS A SIMILAR TEAM OF STARS AND IN A COUPLE OF DAYS
THEY ARE GOING TO PLAY OFF A SERIES BETWEEN THEM, I'M
SURE GOING TO MAKE ONE OF THE GAMES SOMEHOW. IF IT ISNT
TOO LATE MAYBE YOU COULD GET MEL AND BOB TO TAKE YOU T O
A RED SOX GAME I SHOULD THINK IT WOULD BE FUM FOR YOU.
FINNALLY GOT THE BOX OFF TO YOU, TO INSURE
IT I HAD TO HAVE IT IN A BOX AND IT TOK A LITTLE TIME
TO MAKE IT.
GUESS THAT IS ABOUT IT FOR NOW HONEY WISH I
HAD MORE NEWS AND STUFF. ANYWAY DARLIN G IT GIVES ME
ANOTHER CHANCE TO TELL YOU I LOVE YOU WITH ALL MY HEART
AND WITHOUT YOU LIFE WOULDNT BE WORTH A DAM,YOUR EVERY
THING TO ME AND I WANT TO BE BACK IN YOUR ARMS AND
HAVE YOUR LOVE.

BOB

V-MAIL

*just been married, then old jimmied ford ride to the ferry
and Warners hot springs, all the wonderful days of our
honeymoon and in Coronado, coming home to you from
our long trip, then cross-country and the grand times
around home and Boston, deciding to have little Anne and
what a wonderful little tike she is and what wonderful
love she came from. Diego, Norfolk, New York, Phil, then
that long wait and finally home again and the grandest
few months ever, every day honey you grow sweeter and
sweeter and I love you more and more. Won't be long
again darling and I'll be home again and in your arms
and everything will be milk and honey and on our
honeymoon again.*

*Give little Anne a great big kiss and wish her happy
birthday from her old man and say I'll be home again real
soon. Another great big kiss for you too mommie I love
you so and after all its really your day and she is just as
sweet and grand as you honey. I come in there somewhere
but guess all the hell raising is on my side.*

*Not much news honey, squad getting along good. A
little sore about the long delay but still kind of happy
about the big deal. The rank all above JG got a terrific
beating today at baseball from the ensigns. Don't know
how I'll stand up under all this exercise but so far feel
pretty good and think maybe its good for me. Anyway
there's nothing to get in trouble here anyway and even the
bar is closed at six so guess my sweet I'll be a Tarzan by
the time I get back.*

*Beautiful nights here and pretty near full moon and
hate to spend them flying, thinking of you honey and
guess my flying gets a little ragged. Better close for now
be sure and give Annie big kiss and the great big one is
for you. Night sweetie I love you.*

Bob

# # #

Anne and I visited Wo for a week in the fall, and I was
pleased that once again we got along well—I suppose because this
was a visit and not sharing a house. We also spent a weekend in
Newton with the Paulys, and those trips made a welcome break
in the monotony. Aside from that life settled into a very
unexciting routine. Christmas of 1944 came and went. I sent Bob
the usual shoe box of useless trivia, and he sent me that lovely
square amethyst bracelet and two sets of table mats he made to
pass the time at Pearl; one, the red ones I always use at
Christmas and the other, a gray set with a stencil of the VFN 90
insignia, same as the original drawing of the Bat Lady that hangs

in the den.

# # #

Darling,
  *My day off and spent it in a very lazy fashion. Got
up about ten, wondered over for breakfast and shot the
bull with most of the gang. We have a sort of breakfast
club as it's all night fighter pilots at that time. After a
while there I went back to the room and had a few beers
just to prove it was a day off and didn't have to worry
about flying. About 1330 got some of my gang and went
to the final series game. Had a swell time only Army won
the game. The series ended with Navy winning 6 and
army, 1. Returned to the O Club in time for drink before
dinner, etc. and took in the station movie.*
  *Not much news, honey. The squadron doing well.
Going out for night landings on the 9th which should do us
lots of good. Flying these last few nights has been a
picnic with the big moon. Seems bigger out here for some
reason. Anyway it's not something for me to look at
without you except as an assist for our night work.*
                        Love you—you know how much

                        23 October
My darling Anne,
  *First morning I have been up in a long time before
1000. Feels good and also had a real breakfast for a
treat.*
  *Had a letter from Mother with the new pictures. Don't
know why but every time I go away you do the darndest
things to your hair. That fuzzy-wuzzy hair do! Anyway,
its always the way I like it by the time I get home.*
                        Love you just the same,

The winter wore away slowly. I had no close friends in East
Longmeadow or Springfield. My one good friend from Smith
with whom I had had so many good times had also married a
Naval officer and was doing the same thing as the rest of us
Navy wives—chasing him whenever she could. If I remember, all
the while I was in East Longmeadow she was, ironically, in
Coronado. Gas, of course, was rationed. When Bob was on leave,
there was no limit as to what he could get, but for me alone
there was an A sticker on the car which meant approximately
five gallons a week on which I really couldn't do a lot of
gallivanting. Bob's mother would babysit for me every other
Friday so I could take the bus into the mighty metropolis of

I don't think it looked so bad.

Springfield to get my hair done and perhaps have lunch—though alone it was a pleasant change from eating with one hand and stuffing strained liver and carrots into Anne's mouth with the other.

I know I shouldn't have looked a gift horse in the mouth, but I did get completely frustrated with Bob's family. They were very concerned about Bob, but had absolutely no concept of what he was going through, or of conditions under which people were functioning due to the war. Nothing had changed for them except for having me and Anne, which actually was no small thing. Springfield Bronze and Aluminum Co. made parts for Pratt & Whitney, and therefore Bob's dad had priorities for everything; all the gas he wanted, and if he had to travel he could always bump a civilian off a plane, or get a lower berth on a train. But what really teed me off was the fact that they bought food through the black market. When others were elated to find lamb for stew they ate the tenderest loin lamb chops and steaks whenever they wanted. These were ruined for me because they liked steak so well done that it tasted like the sole of an old shoe. On one of my rare shopping forays I found some baby beef liver and brought it triumphantly home, but Bob's mother fed it to the dogs; nothing but calves liver for the McCulloughs.

Went to the movies once that winter, the only time I've gone by myself, to see The Fighting Lady, a documentary on the Yorktown, Bob's first ship. I recognized many people in it, and it was a traumatic experience, complicated by the fact that as I walked into the theatre something blew in my eye. I couldn't get it out and my eye wept copiously all through the movie—must have looked weird, sitting there crying harder than Alice in Wonderland when she almost drowned in her own tears. A kind man in Steiger's optical department removed it after the movie.

14 November

My darling,

Almost could call this a night off. We were all chased down tonight by the Army searchlights for some of their exercises.

Squadron doing fine. Had the usual accidents but nothing to worry about. Harry put on his third wheels up landing and is at present in the dog house. Young's minor auto trouble turned into his getting a contempt of court, and he raised a bit of hell so I've got him restricted, and he is a bit sore. Still getting complaints because the guys in JOQ are making too much noise. Went over myself the other night and helped them so can't say much and look the other way when some makes a fuss.

Darling, I think of you all the time and love you more and

100

more.
Bob

28 November

My dearest wife,
It's so darned beautiful outside, honey. These moons
are the biggest, fullest and brightest you'll ever see. It's
nice and quiet and I have been out on the porch having a
goodnight drink and day dreaming of you.
Been sort of taking it easy after the wild party last
night in town. Started the morning out with a few beers,
flew a couple of hours this afternoon. Had a good supper
and feel pretty fair. A goodnight's rest will see me right
chipper in the morning.
Party was a good one and had a rip snorting time for
myself. All the boys enjoyed it and show it today. About
250 all together all the way from an admiral all the way
down. Had a nice meal and show and a good colored band
for the dancing. The Outrigger Club is very swank and
sits right on you know what beach. An open dance floor
which was okay between showers—first a full moon and
then pouring down rain. Highlight of the party was Tex
doing a novelty dance of his own between showers—. Had
to stop serving the drinks at 1830, but we still got through
ten cases and then started on our own which for some
reason is legal. Guess its the last of the parties until the
break in San Diego next spring.
Be in my new home, I think, on the day before
Mother's birthday and sure hope we can get on our way
right soon.
Think I'll turn in honey. Got a meeting on early in the
morning. It's quite a struggle to get up now even when I
get to bed early. What a habit to form. Guess you'll have
trouble with me trying to get me back to normal.
> *Good night, my darling, sweet*
> *dreams,*
> *I love you*

Bob told me the following story several years later. He had
run into Tom Blackburn somewhere on Barber's Point several
days before the above mentioned party and in a burst of
brotherly-in-law-ly affection had invited him to join them at
same. Tom came and in his true, sadistical sense of humor
returned their hospitality thusly. He, as did everyone else,
imbibed freely and then disappeared. When it was noticed that he
was gone every one became concerned and went to look for him
to find his clothing folded and piled neatly under a palm tree on
the beach—with watch, rings and wallet placed squarely on top

of the pile. The only conclusion they could come to was that he had decided to take a swim and had been somehow swept out to sea. Every one was horrified and there was much milling and stewing around trying to figure out what to do without arousing the authorities. After watching their discomfort for a while, Tom stepped out calmly and nakedly from behind a neighboring palm. Luckily, Bob and his men went to sea shortly thereafter so who knows what they would have perpetrated on Tom in justifiable retaliation.

16 December

My darling,

Just about that time, honey, for me to call it a day. Taking the whole gang in for x-rays tomorrow before we head out to sea. Looks awfully early, and it will be sort of unusual to see the sun come up.

No flying today or tomorrow so we can put the finishing touches on our planes. Things in general look pretty good. Gear goes tomorrow and ourselves on Friday. Looks as if we might have Christmas night ashore, but that will just about end things here for us. Going to miss your swell letters, honey, but they will get to me fairly soon. I'll be right on the gangway to catch Speed when he brings it over. By the way I just made Speed a yeoman first class a week ago.

Not much change in the old gang I brought out. All in all I now have 60 officers and 47 men. Thirty-four planes and the Bat Lady. She has become quite famous as our original planes went out in combat when we first arrived, and they all had the redhead aboard.

Trying to think back to some of your recent letters. Seems to me I was going to answer some questions. Wish I could say something nice about going out to stay with Betty. It would be swell, darling, but I don't think it would be for the best. There is just too much travel and trouble for you, and my plans are so indefinite, and we couldn't possibly travel home together, and there's no telling where my next duty will be. I'm sure Al will be home soon and that would mix things up more. I hope things are nice for you at home, I do want you to be happy. I know it isn't all milk and honey, darling, but we'll make up for everything when I get home.

Darling, you are in my thoughts
always

19 December

My darling,

Been sitting here dreaming, honey, and wishing, too,

and all of it was of you. Gee, how I hate to think that even this little chance to get together will be lost to us in a few days, and we'll have long waits and empty mailboxes.

Hope I won't be an old man, honey, but if things keep on like the last couple of days, I'll lose at least my sense of humor. This damn party business has put me in a lot of hot water, and me and my effort to keep the boys from getting burned and my big mouth and temper, I really told a few people off. At least I have the gang all clear and now just have to talk myself out.

The enlisted men's party was, as you might guess, a humdinger. Spent all my time there breaking up rows and fights, and when the thing finally broke up, I was pretty well tired of it all and had aged ten years. They went through 70 cases of beer. The hula show and food didn't arrive until after dark about two hours late. They rigged some arc lights, and everything finally went along okay.

After I'd finished my letter to you last night and had turned in who should come knocking at my door but Captain Griffin saying my gang was having a riot in JOQ, and the marines had been called in to stop them. So I went over, and you should have seen the place. They really tore it up—I guess as a farewell party. Anyway, we are all in the doghouse. Can't get very excited about it myself—only sorry I wasn't in on it. Hate to think what will happen Thursday our last night ashore. There is a guard on it at present so suppose they will tie him up and really go to town.

Sure do love you, honey
Bob

24 December

My darling,

Just time for a line while we are waiting to take off. Everything in good shape and eager to get started. Will give the field a good buzz like at Charlestown.

Have several of the fighters and torpedo planes all painted up for Christmas. My plane has a big Santa Claus on one side and reindeer on the other. Very snappy as long as I don't end it up in the admiral's lap.

Had a great knockout party last night and will write you about it when I am not sitting on the waiting line to take off.

Love you, honey

# # #

Even though I lived with Bob's family for so many months, I

never did learn much about their family background except that they came from good old New England stock. Bob was the second of three boys, and typical of the middle child was the most conscientious, most generous, and most ambitious. When he graduated from high school he wanted to go on to college, but his father thought it a waste of time so Bob worked for a couple of years to save enough money to start. He enrolled at Springfield college in 1934, but in order to afford it worked a full night shift at nearby Westinghouse while going to classes by day. He even played football, making varsity quarterback in his sophomore year. However, he couldn't keep up that pace, so when the opportunity arose he enlisted in the new Aviation Cadet program at Squantum and went from there to Pensacola for his actual flight training. I've forgotten his rating at Squantum—seaman second class, I guess, or whatever was the lowest he could have been. When he was released in 1945 he had risen to the rank of full Commander, which ain't bad for nine years' service.

27 December
At sea

My darling,

Well, honey, hear I am and so darned busy really don't know if I'm coming or going. When I said I'd write you a letter once aboard and squared away, I didn't know what I was talking about. Honest, honey, I haven't sat still for ten minutes since we landed on board. The only time I have any rest or peace is when I'm in the air, and I'm sure going to take lots of flights just to get away from the confusion. It is expected, of course, to start with, and all in all everything is fine and dandy, and the boys look really good, but right now they come to me for everything. I almost have to put most of them to bed at night and sing them to sleep. There is no time for fooling, and by the time you read this I'll have made men of them and old men, too.

We left the base one jump ahead of the base police and a sure court martial for me. Still in a jam because of their wrecking the JOQ, and, of course, our last night there they wrecked it again, and, boy were the base police after me early in the morning. Luckily for me I sneaked away over here and left them holding the bag. One thing you can be sure our gang will always have spirit.

This will probably be the last letter for a couple of weeks, but don't worry. Everything is okay, and I'll write again as soon as they give us time.

I love you so much, honey
Bob

104

These are copies of an illicit journal handwritten by one of the enterprise's enlisted men.

USS Enterprise CV(N)-6
-1-

(When the Big E sailed again on Christmas eve Dec. 24, 1944 she had a new skipper, a new exec, a new admiral, a new air group and a new designation. She was no longer the USS Enterprise (CV6) but the USS Enterprise CV(N)-6—the Big E was a night carrier, flying a night radar air group—the first carrier to be assigned such duty). Her "new" admiral was tall, hawk-faced Mat Gardner, who a year before had been her captain. Admiral Gardner's operations officer was Roscoe Newman, who a year before had commanded her air group and later had been her assistant air officer. The "new" air group commander was Bill Martin, exec of old scouting 10 in 1942, and skipper of torpedo 10 six months ago, and in maritime night air group ninety were more than a dozen names familiar to the Big E.

In the month of January 1945, Bill Halsey commanding the third fleet, flew his four-star flag in the last Battleship New Jersey.

# # #

These letters were all written during Bob's first month of night fighter combat. Since they all start and end the same, I have omitted their salutations and closings.

This first letter dated 7 January, 1945 was written the day after he went over the side of the Enterprise. His crash landing destroyed one plane on the flight deck and knocked another into the drink ahead of him. He perhaps wrote it while on the Frank waiting to be returned to the Enterprise, but, of course, could tell me nothing.

His flight logbook reads:

Jan 6, 1945 TYPE OF MACHINE F6F-5E; NUMBER OF MACHINE 711110 DURATION OF FLIGHT 5.0 HOURS. CHARACTER OF FLIGHT—STRIKE—LUZON REMARKS —ONE WATER LANDING.

Excerpt from journal:

air group ninety's first strike was not an outstanding success. Three of the fifteen night fighters, because of faulty radar, hydraulics and just plain getting lost, never made the target, but a dozen did. Bob McCullough as squadron commander on a first mission was badly shot up. He attempted a no flap hydraulics, poor throttle—control landing, and went through all the barriers, damaged several planes, knocked one overboard and followed it himself. Four men of the flight deck crew were injured. Fire broke out in the port gun galley. McCullough was picked up at once, bruised and scratched, and was picked up by destroyer, and returned aboard the Enterprise. The rest of their returning planes had to land on the Independence and Lexington carriers, while the Big E cleared her deck and repaired her carrier deck. The pilots that landed on the Lexington were cordially received by the redoubtable famous pilot "Dog Smith" and his air group, back again in the fight for the Philippines.

His next flight wasn't until Jan 12.

7 January
At sea—supporting Luzon
landings

I think of you always. Our love is so strong and without you I just couldn't keep going. Coming home to you and Anne is all I pray for. It's hell, Anne, and I've never been really scared before the way I am now. Some how I keep plugging along, and always your love keeps me

The "Franks' Home for Dripping Aviators" Club

Know Ye That Lieutenant Commander R. J. McCullough, USNR

ON THE Sixth DAY OF January 1945 ABRUPTLY APPEARED INTO

OUR HAPPY HOME, AND DUE TO THE PECULIARITIES OF HIS ARRIVAL, HAS

BEEN FOUND WORTHY OF BEING HONORED AS A Franks Drippy Aviator

BIG DRIP: Commanding Officer

LITTLE DRIP: Executive Officer

going. I'm not worried so much for what happens to me,
but when I think of you and little Anne, I know I must get
through all right.

We're in this in a big way now, and it's a nightmare.
Somehow we just keep slugging along and doing what's
asked and expected. How, I don't really know except the
gang are all the best in the world. We have taken quite a
beating but are still intact though a little bruised. Have a
few flags of the Rising Sun on our planes now and hope
to have more. We are right in the thick of things. When it
quiets down some will write a little better than this. I only
have a few minutes each day.

I can't tell you what's in my heart, honey except I'll
love you always.

The writer of this epic poem made up for his lack of poetic
finesse with his sincerity.

THE NIGHT IS OURS
("Likewise Zero-Zero Days")
'Twas a dark and stormy night out there—
The sea rose masterfully,
And strove to fill with deep despair
The fighting heart of Bull Halsey.

"You're helpless on a night like this"—
"Who's helpless?" roared the Bull!
"Such weather is my favorite dish—
I'm glad the moon's not full!"

"Of course my day groups couldn't fly;
Ceiling low and waves too high—
There must be someone I could send
To search the seas to the very end."

Then fiery flame from his nostrils blew,
And the gleam did light his eye—
His laughter boomed forth deep and mighty—
"Thank God, there's always Air Group 90!"

Now the Fast Carrier Force of our John Sidney
Was so delightful he ruptured a kidney,
With wrinkles smoothed, he turned to Thatch
And said, "Jimmy, my boy, take a dispatch!"

"Old Mathias is my man,
And Willing William, too.
They'll agree to any plan—

To them the sky is always blue!"

Doctrines new were ever spread
By valiant missionaries—
Roscoe from Pasco and Captain Ted
Are now the Fleet's night visionaries.

For they're the ones behind the schemes
Who dream these wild fantastic dreams,
"Now there's a post I'd like to share,"
Mused I, tossed high by their nightmare.

All these oracles to plan
The job for Mac and Kip,
Whose nameless pilots grope to man
Their planes on a darkened ship.

Who cares if this plane won't go,
Engine out—no radio,
It's still an "up"; I ought to know
'Cause Air Plot has just told me so.

"Stand by to start the engines on planes of this flight—"
In cockpits busy hands found switches, with never a
glimmer of light.
"Stand clear of propellers"—still thumbs down—
"Start engines!"—then Bob's voice was drowned.

Spitting, sputtering engines gasped
Some leaped to instant life,
And a throaty, thundering roar at last
Engaged the wind's bold blast in strife.

Taxi down a wave washed deck
And give your mags a careful check—
There's someone there knee deep in brine—
Neptunus Rex, with wands that shine.

Left brake, right brake, tail wheel locked—
'Forward, backward—let the ship rock!
Blinking lights say you're in the gear—
Lord—I must have been trying a year!

Unperturbed by aircraft missions,
Willie Kabler stands—
Starting his brooms and setting conditions,
Keeping house as best he can.

Wings spread, flaps down—one look around
Isn't there some way to give it a down?
There's the wind-up—give 'er the gun—
Lights on—head back—and a 60-foot run.

Whrump! You gasp, and strain for the wheels.
Altitude, gyro, airspeed, heading—
Believe what they tell you,
Not how it feels.

Just below, the wild waves leap,
Licking their chops hungrily
Maybe I do have 300 feet—
But they look awfully close, to me!

A cylinder misses, you're due for a splash
Why worry—after all,
You'll be picked up in just a flash
Says Captain G.B.H. (to us, "Bud") Hall.

One look outside—Lord it's black—
I sure wish I were back in the sack.
Where are the others? Rendezvous, Hell!
If I keep from spinning I'm doing damn well.

What was the message from Com 3rd Fleet?
"The night is yours—good luck—Godspeed—
The prize is there—go grab it—"
Secretly, I think he added—
"Frankly Brother—you can have it!"

ENTERPRISE and Her NIGHT AIR GROUP.

9 January
At sea

For the first time in days, now, I've finally found myself with some free time and a free night ahead! I think. At present there is such really bad weather even the night fighters can't tackle it.

You wouldn't believe it possible if I could tell you where we are and under what conditions we are operating.

It's a screwy life we lead and tougher than I could ever have dreamed of. Scares me most of the time, and about all that keeps me in front where I belong when the going gets tough is knowing all those kids believe in me, and I can't let them down. They have been going through hell these last few days and are all coming through with flying colors. The Ace so far is Neilson with three.

Also our night schedule calls for us shifting our time around so our breakfast is at 1500 and other meals falling in line all around the clock. Been flying day and night and in general so tired don't know whether coming or going. All the boys you know are doing fine.

I think of you always, and when I return I'll tell you all the things I can't write now.

> 12 January—(French Indo-China,
> Camranhba, Cape Hiron-Delle,
> Saigon & Dratos Reef)
> At sea

At last getting chance to get mail off to you. Haven't had any luck receiving any from you, but the way we're moving about don't expect anything for some time.

I'm awfully tired tonight, honey. We've been fighting pretty furiously and we haven't had any sleep for two days. Been staying awake by taking benzedrine which really keeps me going, but finally going to sleep tonight as soon as I finish this. It's sure grim, darling, and the toughest time of my life. Wish I could tell you, honey, some of the things that flash through my mind when I see flashes all around. I only know you are on my mind all the time, and I think only of you and pray for the day when we'll be together again.

> 19 January—(Hong Kong,
> Canton)
> at sea

Don't have a bit of news I can write. Seems like a million years since August and a million more until next June.

It's just plain hell out here, and the worst is watching those youngsters who don't give a damn but get hurt worst of all. It's too late to bring them all back, but each night I pray I'll be able to have all of us together when it's time for us to go home. Think maybe the hardest part is over now. Everyone has been into battle. Having to learn how and to do battle at the same time made it so much tougher.

We have been through plenty of troubles and taken our beating as well as made a fine showing, and I think we are now headed for a short rest and hope next time we will be veterans.

111

Excerpt from journal

*In the afternoon, twelve of Lt. Comdr. Bob McCullough's
VF-90 Hellcats strafed the airfield at Saigon and burned
or demolished five enemy planes, and in the evening four
more F6F's finished off the target.*

-4-

*The next day was the worst of all bad days in the
China Sea—at 8:00 AM the typhoon was 200 miles south
of the Enterprise. A 40-knot wind, heavy swells, and rain
squalls across the Big E deck. The destroyer knifed
through the heavy waves—The big E would go over one big
wave and go through two big waves. In the early afternoon,
Captain Grover B.H. Hall of the Enterprise launched a
strike of avenger and hellcats to destroy un enemy radio
and Weather station on Pratas Reef. A hundred miles
southwest of the force. The first team that took the
mission, Bill Martin, Kip Kippen, and Bob McCullough,
with Charlie Henderson, Ralph Cummings, Ernie Lawton,
Giffy Blake, and C.B. Collins. The group flew all the way
through a series of drumming rain squalls. The dozen
Enterprise aircraft roared and swooped and banked, and
came down to blast and strafe and rocked until nothing
was left of the big concrete installation, except the radio
towers, then Martin Kippen and McCullough went back
down to the water and led their boys home under the
lowering asiatic sky.*

*Jan. 19, 1945, the Big E with TF38 hit enemy
occupied Hong Kont Canton and the island of Hainan. The
weather continued very bad. Of the eight fighters launched
by VF(N) 90 that evening, one inexplicably failed to
return at all, another flew into the water and exploded as
he turned, two crashed the barriers and one landed wheels
up. These are fine crack pilots that are losing their lives.*

First Aid —:—

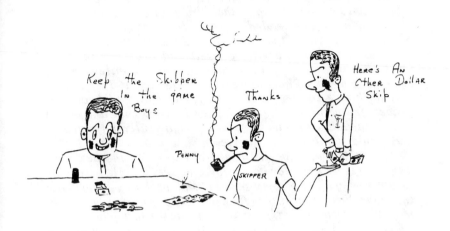

The Morning After —:—

25 January—(Formosa Airfields
Krun Harbot, Okinawa)
at sea

My darling,

I am happier today than I have been for a long time. First, we finally received our first mail, and boy did I rate? I am now caught up to the third of January.

Second we are headed in for a long, hard earned rest. Shouldn't have used the 'long' actually as it won't be over a week, but, anyway, it will be swell and a chance to relax (wet, I hope). The place can't be over a mile long, I expect, and about half mile wide but, boy, it is friendly and a chance to sleep some. Have seen lots of beautiful places from the air lately day and night, sun and moon and rain and dry, but they were all awfully unfriendly, and would you believe it, they even shot at us?

Hope to run into lots of the old gang in the next few days. First of all, plan to run over to see old Al. Also plan to have a squadron party or two, and probably after what the boys have been through will be up for another court martial. Haven't heard from the fuss in the last place.

Have awarded Neilson the DFC and a fellow named Wood the Air Medal. Also Air Medal for Wright. They submitted me for an Air Medal, but I caught it and stopped it as it wasn't for anything real—just a courtesy to CO's, and I figured I would take it later if earned. Isn't that the way we play ball?

Goodnight and sweet dreams
I love you

28 January

My dearest wife,

Good news in a way. The night fighter pilots are only expected to put in four months duty because of the strain, and so with good luck should be through our tour the end of April. Have one hell of a job coming up soon, but guess if we are careful we'll get away with it. Anyway four months of this stuff and I'll be unable to crawl up to the plane let alone fly the darned thing.

The trip to the beach wasn't so hot. First you got all wet on the way in and it usually takes about an hour. Then you fight sixty-thousand aviators for a beer. Then it's time to go back. By this time you're all dry and so get all wet again on the way back, and boy, it's good to be back on the ship again instead of dry land, nuts!

Still carry the weight of the world on my shoulders, but at least now I'm getting a full night's sleep. The boys are all okay and after all things are going all right.

Golly, sure seem to be wound up tonight. Have a tough day tomorrow and have to attend a million meetings. Bill Martin is a swell guy but a little on the official side and is trying to make me over some and somehow or other not having any luck. I'm still nasty and stubborn and still run the squadron any way I think best.

> *Goodnight, my darling,*
> *I love you,*
> *Bob*

3 February,

My darling,

Tonight this letter might turn into anything—a masterpiece or a lark, a note or a volume. As I see it the typing drills I have been taking are doing me a lot of good, and the beer party I just attended has had the same effect. I should be well on my way to dreamland but couldn't turn without writing my honey a word or two. Anyway, you judge for yourself and let me know.

The Air Group has managed another party as you should be able to tell. I had a wonderful time except I didn't quite fold up like the rest of the gang, and as a result, I became a good Samaritan and, I think, got most of them aboard. I expect we left a dozen or so on the beach, but it was dark and we couldn't be expected to find them all. I have seen a lot of parties in my time, honey, but I think this one topped them all. I really don't blame them, but, boy, what a time getting them back—not only the ensigns but a cdr and a captain or two managed to hit the dirt on this happy occasion. Just to make sure every one has had fair chance and not to let the duty boys miss out we are going to have another one tomorrow night. Oh, boy!

It's a shame, really to have parties. The Navy took over the native village and moved them to another island. The officers' section is quite beautiful—huts just like in th movies and the native settlement just as they left it.

Captains' inspection all okay this morning. In fact we were complimented on our fine appearance. I still don't believe it, but I guess it's so.

> *Golly, honey, but I love you and*
> *miss you so much*
> *Bob*

6 February

My darling,

It's that grand time of day when all my work is over. I secure everything and refuse to answer the phone, and anyone wishing to do work must make a trip up here, and then I'm very rude to them, and they soon leave. I just sit around a while thinking of you and Annie and home enjoying my pipe or cigar and just forget that I am way out here at sea away from you, and for a short moment, honey, I am right there in your arms.

My social activities are getting the best of me—feel like my day is just one mad rush, boat trips, soakings and beer. This squadron commander business keeps me on my best behavior and have to make appearances somewhere each day. Bill just eats it up and always drags the VT skipper and me along. We sit around but really don't have much to say. Every trip means a new set of khakis, and damn, but I'm hard put to keep up. The Captain invited us to the beach today for a few beers and then for dinner with him. Got another soaking even in the gig but really had a swell time and a most elegant dinner. Best of all, though, found that the Captain is an old fighter pilot and loves to tell about his heyday and, boy, did I get a chance to outshine Dapper Bill.

Al and I took in the gala premier of The Fighting Lady, and it is really great. You must see it, darling, if it comes to town. It is almost an exact review of my tour of duty out here last year. (Aboard the Belleau Wood)

Be finished here in a few days and think all the boys are in fair shape and had a little rest. The next job will be an eye opener, and we will need all the breaks we can get and lots of guts. Sure hope the gang pulls through.

All the news for this one.
Sure love you, honey
Bob

# # #

Excerpt from the illicit journal kept by one of the Enterprise's enlisted men.

The pilots buckled on their incredible array of gear—their chart boards, knives (machete), revolvers, flashlights, whistles, waterproof charts, flags, vitamins, first aid kits, dye markers, shark repellent, very pistols and flares, compasses, fishing kits, matches, helmets and goggles', oxygen masks, Mae Wests, parachutes and rubber rafts and went back to flying against the enemy at night.

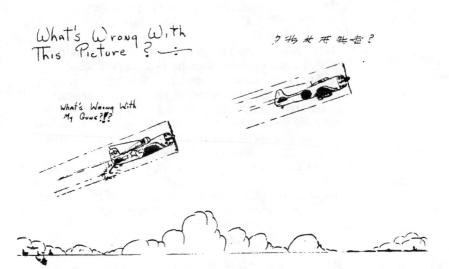

My darling,

Just a little note to maybe get me one ahead when the next mail call catches me unawares as it usually does.

We're so busy, my darling, and the toughest time yet. When I get a few minutes, I have to spend them sleeping. The rest of the time I'm either flying day and night or both and standing by in the ready room sweating the other boys in. Can't say a thing about where we are but maybe will get a chance later on or if not it will all keep til I get home, and then it won't see so bad with you by my side anyway.

Don't know when this silly note will get off, but it is swell taking a few minutes off talking to you, darling.

I love you,
Bob

Excerpt from a letter from Dave Lister, President of the U.S.S. Enterprise Association although we have never actually met we have become good friends through our common interest.

No, as you say, I never knew your Bob, but of course knew who he was, and saw him on an almost daily basis. My entire tenure aboard ENTERPRISE was on the flight deck, and after AIR GROUP 90 came aboard we of the flight deck crew lived about 90% of our hours top-side, more often than not sleeping and eating there, only occasionally did we get below decks for a shower and a "real" sleep. We had many more accidents than normal during that period because everyone was so fatigued. Even though it was tough on us, it was even tougher on the flight crews, and we had the utmost admiration for them, I still do. It wasn't until after the war when I got into aviation myself that I realized what great pilots these guys really were. It took a lot of ability, not to mention guts, to go out and find the enemy and do battle with him, and THEN find your landing field that had moved a couple hundred miles, and get safely aboard. Now imagine duplicating this feat, IN THE DARK, it's still incredible to me. Over the years I wrote to many of the pilots who flew from the deck of ENTERPRISE to let them know time had not diminished their heroic exploits in my eyes. I wish I had known Bob McCullough's whereabouts and written him also. Believe me when I tell you he was a genuine hero . . . but then you are the one person that does not need to be told.

*27 February—(Supporting Iwo
Jima Landings—Iwo Jima
and Haha Jima)*

My darling,
*These days somehow get away from me. This is the
fourth continuous day and night that our squadron has had
planes in the air without a break and no sign of relief in
sight for a few more days. I very seldom see any of the
guys as we are all flying around the clock, and when we
are not flying we are trying to get some sleep. I manage
to get all the rest I need and think most of the gang the
same, but it doesn't give us any time for anything else.
Think, perhaps, it won't be too much longer before we go
back to our little island and maybe have a few days of
relaxation and a few beers.*

*Not doing a very spectacular job but a tough one and
lots of hard flying. Have a few more heroes in the outfit
and some more medals to hand out, but not all milk and
honey and a few tough breaks as well. Trying to stay out
of trouble the best I can, honey. I was up over a target the
other night, watching the battle and listening to a
shortwave broadcast from Frisco telling you people all
about it as well. Sometimes I think you all know more and
get a better overall view than we are able to out of the
action reports.*

*I love you with all my heart,
honey
Bob*

# # #

The winter of 1945 passed slowly; the only things that kept
me going were Bob's letters which were marvelous, but
frustratingly vague. If anything positive was being accomplished
in either the European or Pacific war zones, the authorities kept
it quiet. It seemed Bob had been gone forever and I didn't think
he'd be home until the war was over which, according to the
media, wouldn't be for at least a couple of years.

*11 March
Land ho!*

My darling,
*We are getting into that miserable little island of ours
that the Navy calls home, Ulithe. Sometimes it's hard to
believe that we can stay out for days on a cruise and just
wait for the word that we re on on our way back to it, but
it does mean rest for a while and a few beers. I'm in
terrible shape for need of a good night's sleep but think*

119

Excerpt from journal

When lean outspoken Commander Jack Blitch, perched restlessly on his stool in "Fly Control" high over the Big E's deck, gave the order to launch eight fighters for a dusk CAP over IWO at 4:25 pm, on the 23rd of February, he began a week of operation that no carrier had equaled before. Bill Martin's air group and Jack Blitch's air department split into shifts and settled down to continuous operations until 11:30 pm on the second of March, when a passing warm front smothered Gardner's task group in heavy rain and zero-zero-weather for forty five minutes, there had not been a moment, night or day for seven days and seven hours, that at least two Enterprise planes had not been air borne. Once there were twenty-two; most often there were four to six. Bob McCullough night fighting 90 averaged fifty flights every twenty-four hours.

one and a few beers will fix me up for a while.

Have arranged to take the gang over to the beach for two days. We will hang around and drink beer to our heart's delight. None of the gang exactly cracked this time but pretty near to the point in a few cases because of hard work and lack of sleep. Sure have the best gang in the world. Boy, if this gang were turned loose like the day outfits it would be another turkey shoot. As it is all we do is darned hard jobs under tough conditions at night that wouldn't even pass day time standards.

The official action has gone enough so I don't think the censor will cut out the names again. I thought you would want to know we have lost Saddler, Tex and Wright. Darned tough, as you know and when Tex went, it just about licked the gang. Sure took me in a few tucks, too.

I think you know our dates and time are considerably different, don't you? Roughly, when it is noon for you, it's about 0300 the next day for me or something like that. Don't try to figure it out, but in general I'm a day ahead—mostly. Our day is all mixed up now that we work day and night, and I never even bother to figure days, dates or dark or light. Will certainly take some time to get me straightened when I get home.

Love you with all my heart,

28 March
(March 18-21 Kyushu First
Carrier Strikes inland sea,
Kyushu & Shikoko Airfields,
Kobe)

My darling,

This party life we are leading at present makes me so darned lazy that even as bad as I want to write it's hard to sit down and lift my fingers. I'm getting about 14 hours of sleep, practically no work and parties ashore every afternoon. I've come to the conclusion that a party every other day is my speed. As you can imagine, they're pretty rough. We find a deserted spot on the beach, bring along a couple of cartons of whiskey, some beer, some hamburg, some ice and a few mess boys. Sometimes the ship's band, and away we go until everyone has about passed out. There are no fancy fixings or anyone's feelings to worry about, and it's just clean fun with the sole purpose to relax or better still to collapse. No one knows how long we'll be in and figure better take it while it's available. I surely hate to think of getting started again' and it will take me a good many days to get the gang in shape again.

Golly, honey, there's nothing more to say, but I surely

121

hate to stop because I'm so lonesome and sitting here writing to you helps more than anything else.

> *How I need you and love you*
> *Bob*

29 March

My darling,

This is one of those rainy days you hear about in the tropics. No boats and everyone stuck aboard. Have put in a bare minimum of office work and a couple of hours in a crap game—Came out a big winner. Been pretty bad here the last couple of days, but the rain has made it nice and cool and good for sleeping. Really getting plenty of rest for a change.

Thought that I would enjoy loafing for a bit, but right now I think maybe we have had enough and would like to get out again. Hoping that after the next one they will figure we have had enough and send us home. With that in mind we are having a hard time taking it easy.

> *Not much news, as usual, honey.*
> *I love you so much, but that's*
> *not news.*
> *Bob*

6 April

My darling,

Well, here we go again, honey. Hope by the time this reaches you we'll be through our job and headed toward home. Was sure that we could get in for a spell and get the needed rest. Had time enough this time so that everyone is in good shape and raring to go.

The squadron was one year old yesterday, remember? We had a little anniversary party but not as we would have liked. Being at sea we didn't have any spirits but ice cream and cake. Some changes from when we started. The ready room was jammed full. 64 officers and 51 men and quite a handful to keep going.

All the gang is in good shape also in pretty good spirits. I think mostly because they are planning on this being the last operation and look forward to being home soon. I sure hope so. They have been so swell, but I don't think they could take much more. Phil is still grounded with a broken knuckle, and Harry can't sit down very well because of a piece of lead in the seat of his britches. He has taken a lot of kidding. We are all waiting to see how he is going to explain his purple heart medal.

> *Wish I could tell you, honey,*
> *of all the love in my heart.*
> *Bob*

14 April
(Supporting Okinawa
landings, Okinawa Jakishima,
Gunto, Anami-Gunto

My darling,
Gee, honey, it's nice to say hello again. Been pretty busy and have been sleeping in the ready room. This is the first time in a couple of days I have been back to my room. Looks rather like a long tough deal this trip and don't expect much rest.

No news, honey. The censor restrictions on a good many of our past operations have been lifted, but don't think you would really care for it. Will give you all the stories much better when we can sit down some evening at home later on.

Might just give you an idea of where we have been:
Started with the Philippines invasion
Formosa
French Indo-China
Hong Kong
Canton
Tokyo—two trips
Kyushi—two trips
Iwo Jima invasion.
That is all I'm allowed to say for the present.

Guess I'd better wander back to the ready room to see what's cooking—in the way of flights, I mean. We have been living on battle rations the last couple of days. A good hot meal, a shower and a goodnight's sleep will be welcome.

Honey, did I ever tell you I'm crazy about you?
Bob

15 April

My darling,
Didn't expect to get a breather this soon, but here we are back in our dumpy lagoon and not knowing whether we are up or down or coming or going. Same old story—rumors all over the place and nothing official to back them up. If you take a nap for a couple of hours it takes a couple days to get caught up on all the hot dope that has been passed around in the meantime.

Anyway, whatever happens it's sure swell to be back. Each time we go out it gets tougher. We really haven't been out long this time, but I feel 100 years old and can't remember having any sleep. Last time was the first sleep in 48 hours, and there have been five stretches just like it. Today is the first time I have been in my room for five days.

I love writing to you, and at the same time I sure have taken a funny liking for typing and do it for my recreation. It sidetracks my mind for a while and keeps me from going crazy.

> I miss you so much, my darling
> and want only to come home
> to you
> Bob

19 April

My darling,

Can't even remember how long we have been in but guess I have been neglecting to write.

Had visions of sticking around the ship with nothing to do and had planned on getting a note off each day. As it turned out I decided to come ashore with the gang flying CAP, and here I am roughing it instead.

When I stay aboard, they drive me crazy all day and all night, first this and then that. Here on the island it's rough and dirty, but I'm completely the boss and do just as much as necessary and that's all. Getting a swell change here, and beachcombing isn't so bad.

Here is what it's like. Sleep on a cot in a tent—coconut palms for shade on the beach. Cold water and use a helmet for wash basin. No plumbing except for a Chick Sales. Three foot lizards running all over the place. Flying bats and wild hogs. Once in a while get the courage to shave but only about every three days. Food not bad and plenty of beer and whiskey. Miss breakfast each day and usually have a beer instead of orange juice. Swimming fine they tell me though I haven't tried it yet. Haven't any idea when I'll go back to the ship. Still haven't decided if we are coming or going. However, the odds look as if we'll be going back out for at least another month.

Pretty hot in the daytime and have to be careful not to exercise too much. Get 12 cases of beer each day from the ship and also have talked them out of two cases of Four Roses.

We are not too popular with the Marines here. They turned out the lights on us the other night and broke up a swell party.

Most of the boys are over here with me flying the patrol. Some of them can't take it, or so they claim, so I sent them back to the ship.

Well, honey, guess I should wind this up and go see that the boys aren't in any trouble. Wish I knew when we *are coming home. Can't be more than a month so hang in there, honey, and I will, too.*

> *Love you with all my heart,*
> *Bob*

# # #

Anne and I went to Washington early in May, and it was good to be back among my own kind again. There were lots of Navy friends, some with husbands around and others, like me, existing from letter to letter. Quite unexpectedly VE day came while I was there, which gave us all hope the Pacific war might also be shortened, and I went back to East Longmeadow much heartened.

> *2 May*

My darling,
Here we go into another month. Golly, April was so long I thought it would never end. I'm afraid that May will be the longest of all, and we will have to postpone our June second honeymoon as we will be going out again in a few days. Guess this will really finish us up. It's a long trip, though, so guess you'd better add another month for travel. It has surely been long and tough. Guess we are taking it on the chin and just plain unlucky.

The boys are all in good shape, planes, too, and have had a good long rest so ought to give a good showing and wind everything up in apple eye order.

I'm so darned blue and lonely, but I always kid myself and say just another month and I can do it standing on my head. Just as long as you and Annie are okay and will be there waiting and I can come back to you—that's all that matters, and all this time apart will fade away as soon as we are in each others arms again.

> *Goodnight and sweet dreams*
> *I love you,*

# # #

There had been no letters from Bob and no news about anything in the Pacific for about three weeks, and I was restless and apprehensive.

Bob and his mech on the
flight deck of the
Enterprise.

Bob receiving decoration
on the Enterprise.

November 1944-May 1945.

17 May
At sea
(May 6-11 Amami Gunto, Daits-
Gunte, Kyushu and Shikoku
Airfield)
(Mall To14 Kyushu & Shikoky
Airfields)

My darling,
Not too fond of this typewriter. It's the old wreck in the office. Have no lights in my room and also my typewriter is on the bum. Of all the things in my room it was the only thing to get hurt.

Golly, it's nice to find a free minute to sit down and write. It has been the toughest trip of all and I'm glad it's over.

We are leaving the battle zone for the last time and when you receive this, I'll be well on my way to you, darling. Can't say the date so it's apt to be a week or two either way, honey. Will call you as soon as I can like always.

Fellows did themselves proud this last time and really put us in the big time. We surely have been taking a beating and working like hell but finally broke through and it's a swell feeling for me to know we made good. Will sure have some interesting stories to tell.

Hope to get this off in a couple of days and sure bet it will be good news at last. Golly, I can hardly wait to throw my arms around you and tell you how I've missed you and how I love you.

# # #

Then came an unexpected, and to me miraculous phone call—the Enterprise was in Seattle for repairs! She had been hit by a Kamikaze plane, but fortunately Bob was in the ready room at the time as his quarters were damaged by shrapnel. The old black typewriter in our upstairs storage closet is evidence, also part of one of the cylinders from the Japs plane made into an ashtray.

I learned later the plane, a Zeke went straight down the plane elevator shaft propelling the forward elevator 400 feet in the air and depositing the lifeless body of the pilot, Tomi Zai, at the bottom of the shaft with his calling card in his pocket.

I also learned from one of the radar officers, Blip Vranicar, that he was in the ready room when he heard the frightening roar of the diving plane. He dove for the nearest shelter and when the catastrophic moment was over, he discovered he was crouching for shelter under a glass-topped table.

Excerpt from Journal

Monday the 14 of May at 5:30 we were landing the night CAP. We were at battle stations at 4:30 am general quarters, everyone on the ball. Us lookouts were straining our eyes into binoculars searching the sky. We reported column 4 smoke on the southwest horizon where enemy planes had fallen to the CAP. 6:53. The starboard five-inch guns shook the ship as they opened fire at a single Zeke which broke out of the low clouds 5 or 6 miles away. The Zeke ducked back in the clouds, the 5 inch still banging away at him in full radar control. You could tell the Zeke was after us. We look outs picked him up high in the sky, he came out of a cloud base in a fast-shallow dive, the 20's and 40 mm were on him all the way in, the Enterprise swung to port, the kamikaze continued straight down not jerking at all 35 barrel of 20 mm, 16-40 mm and 4-5 inch guns firing until the whole ship was yellow with smoke on the flag bridge, Jimmy Flatley stepped out to take a look and ducked right back into where the admiral stood yelling "hit the deck". But from the lookout station the pretty, deadly, brown-green Zeke with the big bomb under its belly slanted down over the port quarter. It looked like he was going to slam right into us and the island, the last second he flipped over and dove right through the forward elevator, the bomb went down 5 decks and the Big E's no one elevator, went 400 feet into the sky. It hung for a second then fell back into the sea. Marc Mitcher was the only man standing when the officers staff rose from the deck and began to move out as smoke poured into the compartment. We lookouts could see everyone and everything. The Enterprise was badly hurt. The flight deck was blasted up three feet aft of the demolished elevator. The gasoline system was wrecked, the pressure main crushed, and three or four tanks leaking. The forward guns were out of action there were twenty foot holes in her decks down to the third. Damage control went to work with chief carpenter Walter Woznick and chief bosun's mate "Gabby" Goffareo led rescue and working parties into the flaming five inch gun groups to bring out the dead and wounded. Seventeen minutes after she was hit, Enterprise had her fires under control, and another thirteen minutes they were out. The Big E was down seven feet at the bow, and up three feet at the stern with 2000 tons of water that entered through the ruptured fire main. Thirteen were killed and sixty eight wounded. Eight men who were blown overboard were promptly picked up by the destroyer Walden but chief pilot Tomi

Zai (his body, with calling cards in his pocket as found at the bottom of the elevator well). He was the commander of the famous kamikaze squadron. He knew what he was doing.

When the Enterprise came in, orders were waiting for Bob to report to the air station at Kingsville, Texas, with ten days' leave and travel time. He had his plane tickets and would arrive at Brainerd Field the following day. This time there were no further delays or bumps due to higher priorities, and I was waiting at the gate at arrival time with Anne in my arms and a gardenia in my hair. The plane landed on time and disgorged a mixture of Army, Navy, and Marine corps uniforms, none of them containing Bob. As the last officer went by he must have noticed my stricken expression and said, "Don't give up, there's another plane right behind this one," and there was, in about five interminable minutes, with Bob on it. I could have used our old refrain, "Where in hell have you been?" but I was too happy to speak. He brought me a lovely string of pearls he had picked up at Pearl, and even though we had to share the time with his family, relatives, and friends it was a wonderful leave, and as usual over much too soon.

Bob was going to be instructing in night fighters at Kingsville, and they promised him 18 months of shore duty, unheard-of heaven. Again he wanted me to stay with his family for a month or so until he got settled, but this time I flatly refused. Betty and Al Masters had quarters at Corpus Christi Air Station, and invited Anne and me to stay with them for as long as it took to find a place to live in Kingsville. I did compromise to the extent that Anne and I wouldn't drive with him but would take the train several days later, rather than trying to fly, because although the train took about four times longer, at least we'd be steadily moving ahead instead of sitting in one airport and then another and end up taking a train anyway.

Chapter 10

Bob took off early one morning with all our worldly goods that weren't in storage: my sterling, my cruise box of emergency rations, my red hat, even Anne's little trike. The following Tuesday Anne and I started our trip to Kingsville, Texas, the end of the civilized world. The train came in from Boston about 7:30 p.m. on its way to St. Louis, and Bob's parents took us and our 3 suitcases, 2 coats, my pocketbook, Anne's pocketbook full of small toys, and her security blanket, a large teddy bear, to the station. We could only get an upper berth but were lucky to get that—on all my travels during the war I never had anything but an upper. Could never figure out the requisites for getting a lower; they were always occupied and the occupants looked like just ordinary people. There must have been something special about them—cousin to the President, mistress of a railroad executive?

When the train came in we gaily boarded it only to find someone else in our seats. The conductor said not to worry, he'd straighten it out as soon as the train pulled out. So we left Springfield, Anne and I sitting in the middle of the aisle surrounded by our luggage, and Bob's mother and dad standing on the platform in complete consternation. As promised, the conductor found us another upper which was already made up, so, thinking Anne was probably tired from all the excitement I elected to get ready for bed. Wrong—she was full of pep and raring to go. The ladder to the upper berth intrigued her, and she went up and down innumerable times before it lost its appeal. Every time I'd get her settled down, someone would walk down the aisle talking and Anne would pop her head over the curtain and say hi. Everyone but her mother thought she was adorable. Finally the lights went out, people stopped talking, and we both went to sleep.

The next three days spent on various trains were interminable. As soon as there was any noise Anne would be up, greeting everyone in sight. Then we'd struggle for half an hour trying to dress in the confined space of an upper, almost impossible for two people when one was such a wiggleworm. We'd wait in line for the rest room and then for the dining car, where Anne never ate a complete meal but nibbled just enough to give her boundless energy. I'd try to get her to take a nap after lunch, but she'd keep going until about 4 p.m., then sleep so hard I'd have to wake her to get to the dining car before it closed. Anne was allergic to eggs and orange juice, but they were the only things on the menu she wanted. Strangely enough, by the time we got to Corpus, the eczema they usually gave her had disappeared.

The weather was hot all through the southeast and the air

conditioning very primitive, so the heat was unbearable. At certain stops they'd fill a large metal box on top of each car with ice, and soon the car was so cold we had to put our coats on. As the ice melted the air inside grew warmer and stickier until we were back to where we'd started.

We got to St. Louis at 6 p.m. on a Wednesday, and the temperature was 106 degrees. I loaded Anne, our three suitcases, two coats, two pocketbooks, and one teddy bear into a taxi and directed the driver to a new Statler hotel which I knew had just opened. We got a heavenly, air-conditioned room, beautifully furnished. We each took a long, soaking bath, and then enjoyed a marvelous dinner brought to us by room service. Anne ate all she could—they didn't have children's portions then.

It was so delightfully relaxing we hated to leave. Our train left for Houston at midnight, and I had asked a train official what time it could be boarded, and he said around 9:30. The station had been so crowded when we arrived at 6 p.m. that I hoped to avoid the hassle by getting aboard as early as possible so I gathered up Anne, me, our three suitcases, two coats, two pocketbooks, and one teddy bear and back to the station we went. Much to our surprise, it was almost completely deserted. I found the gate from which the train left, but, of course, there was no train there. With all that luggage it was a little difficult to do much wandering around so I had the porter deposit us and all our accouterments on a waiting room bench as close to the gate as possible. Time dragged itself by, and as it did the station gradually started to fill up, and as 11:30 and the train arrived, it was, per usual, wall to wall people. The train was finally announced, and of course, by that time Anne had fallen asleep, and there wasn't a porter to be found. I carried her and the coats, pocketbooks and teddy bear in my arms and started the long process of pushing the suitcases ahead of us with my feet.

All during the war there was such a feeling of togetherness and camaraderie. Hard to describe without seeming mawkish and sentimental, but everyone was fighting for a common cause, and we all believed with all our hearts that we were united to save ourselves and our country from the world forces of evil. Sorry to sound so melodramatic, but that's the way it was. All of which is leading up to the fact that in a couple of minutes two G.I.'s joined me. One took Anne, the other, the luggage. They helped us through the crowd and to our new upper berth. During the rest of the trip they came from their troop car periodically to be sure Anne and I were okay until they were switched to a train going to San Anton.

We got into Houston about 8:00 Friday morning. Houston was hotter than St. Louis had been, but there was a fairly respectable looking hotel across the street so Anne and I, the three suitcases, two coats, two pocketbooks, and the teddy bear safaried across the street with the help of the porter, and they said we could have a room if we'd be out by noon. That was all we wanted it for, anyway, so we happily moved in. The room had been very hastily cleaned up, and there was a leftover tie draped across the bureau. It was black and cotton and therefore one that nobody in the world but a U.S. Naval officer would have worn so I assumed that was who had been the previous occupant of the room.

Anne was splashing contently in the tub, and I was spreadeagled in a chair thoroughly enjoying the air conditioning and the soft upholstery, when the phone rang. I thought, "O god, they're going to kick us out and we'll have to wander the station again until 12:00 as of Wednesday night." There was silence when I first said hello, but then a slightly agitated female voice asked if Dick was there, the owner of the tie no doubt. I was so upset myself that I guess I did rather an unkind thing. instead of explaining how come I was there, I just said sweetly, "I'm sorry he's not here right now" and hung up. After 40 years I apologize and hope I didn't break up a beautiful romance.

We went back across the street to the station at 11:30, and it was just like all the other stations we had been in, but again along came a kind Navy enlisted man. He was going to Corpus, too, so helped us get settled, no reservations, this was an all coach train, but with his help we had no difficulty. He sat next to us, had a child of his own about Anne's age, and so he and she entertained each other all afternoon until she fell asleep about 4:30, of course, since we were due in at 5.

The train arrived on time. No need this time for "Where in hell have you been?" And it was so good to see Bob and the Masters waiting for me on the platform, and, though we didn't know it—it was projected that the war in the Pacific would go on for another two years—thus began our final tour of duty.

Chapter 11

The Masters had very nice quarters, no air conditioning, but only hotels, offices, and theatres had it in the early forties. It was large and airy and on the second floor so they got what breeze there was—a prevailing wind off the gulf of Mexico. It came up about 4 every afternoon and blew until dark straight through the apartment, not a cool wind, but at least it stirred up the air and at times blew so hard it cleaned out the ash trays and blew the butts and dust curls (Think I've mentioned that Betty's housekeeping was somewhat on the casual side) into little piles on the leeward side of the apartment where they could easily be swept out the door. The wind was an inexpensive cleaning woman.

There was a large commissary on the station, but even it was hard put to keep well stocked shelves; so many people, and rationed foods were getting harder and harder to get,—no fresh oranges and in the midst of cattle country, practically no beef. Betty asked me if Anne liked fish which she did, so one day she came home with three or four little silvery things that looked rather like grunion. They were cleaned but had their heads and tails still on. To be sure they stayed fresh, Betty stuck them in the refrigerator freezer which in those days was just a small box large enough for 4 ice trays and maybe a couple of quarts of ice cream. She stuck them in head first, and as we never seemed to get around to defrosting them in time to use them, forever after when anyone opened the freezer to get ice he was greeted by four stiffly frozen little fish tails.

It was a 50-mile drive for Bob to come from Kingsville so after the first week or two he slacked off and came only 2 or 3 times a week which I found quite upsetting. It was so hot in Texas in June and July that no one went out between 10 and 3. There was a pretty pool, but everyone said even with the chlorine, the temperature was so high that the pool was unhealthy. We went once (taking Anne, of course) with such dire results we never went again. Even the drinking water and the pasteurized milk were not deemed safe, and I was taking Anne to the dispensary for typhoid shots. The day after her second shot and also the day after our swim in the pool, she awoke feeling rather cranky. She got progressively worse as the morning wore on, but I thought it was reaction to the shot and so didn't pay much attention although her temperature rose to 104 degrees, until suddenly she went into a convulsion. I had never seen one before and was scared to death.

There was only one pediatrician on the station for some thousand children, and to get him on the phone you just had to dial over and over til you managed to hit between calls. Fortunately I only had to dial twice, and he said to put Anne in

How Bob spent the Hurricane.

BIG
PROFESSIONAL **BULL FIGHT**

VILLA ACUÑA, MEXICO.
(ACROSS FROM DEL RIO, TEXAS)

SUNDAY SEPT. 2nd. · 5 P.M.

Presenting the
two best
matadors of
the season
here.

JULIAN PASTOR IDOL OF MEXICO

IN COMPETITION WITH

RUTILO MORALES

FIGHTING TO DEATH

4 PURE SPANISH BLOODED BULLS 4

DINE AND DANCE AT "LA MACARENA" CAFE & BAR

a tub of cool water, and then when she revived to take her to the hospital on the base, which we did. There was no children's ward, just a large room with two or three cribs. They wouldn't let me stay but said they were going to start her on penicillin (still used just by the service and not released to civilians). So I went unhappily home and tried to get hold of Bob who was, naturally, out on a flight from Kingsville, I left a message telling him she was in sick bay with a temperature of 104°. He called us soon as he got in, but not me, the hospital, and so marvelous were the powers of penicillin that by the time he called her temperature was down to normal, and he then called me and raked me over the coals for making such a mountain out of a molehill.

She recovered in a couple of days and things were just returning to normal when a hurricane was reported on its way up the gulf and heading straight for our area. As always the Navy had no thought for dependents, but was concerned with getting men and equipment out of the hurricane's path. Al had a desk job so he stayed where he was, but Bob and the rest of the pilots at Kingsville betook themselves and their planes to Del Rio right on the Mexican border and out of harm's way (from hurricanes, that is). They had a marvelous 3-day vacation tippling and gambling while those of us who were left at Corpus faced the worst winds and rain I ever hope to see.

Around noon the sky started to get cloudy, it was hot and sultry and very still, but as the afternoon wore along the wind started blowing progressively harder and harder, and the rain started to fall. Everything kept increasing in volume, but I didn't want Anne to be upset so I put her to bed, though in a room to the lee of the wind. She slept peacefully through the whole night even when I picked her up and moved her from bedroom to bedroom (3 of them) as the wind shifted. Strangely enough neither the electricity nor the phones went out all during the course of the storm. By ten o'clock the wind was blowing over a hundred miles an hour, so hard that the heavy rain was falling (if you could call it that) parallel to the ground and therefore into the sides of whatever buildings were in the way. The quarters were all made of stucco, and the rain hit them with such force that it penetrated them and ran in rivulets down the inner walls. Al and I mopped frantically and did manage to keep ahead of it. Betty thought the whole thing futile and refused to take part. The rain also forced its way in wherever the wires entered the house and ran along them. There were several lights hanging from the ceiling, chandeliers with bowls for shades. The dripping rain soon filled them to overflowing, but we really didn't dare touch them so just put bowls under the bowls and let the water splash merrily away.

Around midnight the fire siren started to blow and went on

Bob with his three stripes and scrambled eggs—October 1945.

seemingly forever. There was a German P.O.W. compound on the station, and we though perhaps they had escaped (though it was said they were all content and didn't want to be released or sent home). Then we thought perhaps it was warning of a tidal wave, horrible thought, even more so because we could look right out over the gulf from the living room. Fortunately, this turned out to be false, too. The system had short circuited, and it had taken some half an hour to get it turned off.

By that time the wind had shifted around to the north and west, and either wind and rain had slackened or we had become so used to the sound and fury that we didn't notice it so much, so I picked up Anne and went to bed in one of the bedrooms on the east side of the house.

The next morning was the most beautiful one I saw while we were in Texas, clear blue sky and cool temperature. Surely was a mess underfoot though, branches, shingles blown from heaven knows where, broken glass. As a point of interest, even Admiral Rock couldn't get through to the base by phone, to find out how his daughter who lived in the same block as the Masters was, but somehow Bob's dad managed it, and was very relieved to find us still in one piece, though I couldn't tell him anything about Bob.

We were warned to boil all water before drinking it, but unfortunately Anne drank some that was contaminated and came down once more with a sore throat and high fever. This time the pediatrician really went all out, Penicillin and sulfa and aspirin and lots of liquids. I was able to care for her at home but had to make out a written chart to keep her dosages straight. I was giving her something every half hour. Fortunately, her resistance was remarkable, and with the help of the whole medicine cabinet she threw off the infection in not too long a time though she never was her really perky self until we left the revolting climate that was Texas.

About that time Bob and Al both made full Commander, 3 lovely gold stripes on their sleeves and gold spinach or scrambled eggs or whatever on their cap visors (Bob's dress blues, cap, medals, sword, aviator greens, naval records and a machete issued when he was flying over the jungled islands of the Pacific, are all together in the storage closet upstairs. As are all the letters he wrote while at sea.)

Chapter 12

Bob was still living at the B.O.Q. in Kingsville and Anne and I with the Masters in Corpus Christi when suddenly one day the war was over. Bob came over, and the Masters and we toasted anything and everything with Anne's Hague and Hague pinch bottle. We had all lived in the shadows of uncertainty, war and death (couldn't and wouldn't want to list the numbers of friends we had lost to the machinations of war) that our minds really couldn't take in the fact that it was finally over.

Bob definitely wanted to return to civilian life, but since nobody knew how long it would be before he could, he found a little house for us in Kingsville, and for the next to the last time I gathered up all our possessions, including my sterling silver and the emergency cruise box, the red hat and Anne, and off we went. Didn't have Willie with us as transportation for him from Springfield to Corpus had been practically impossible. I had felt very badly about leaving him, he had been my good friend and companion all during the war when Bob was gone, and I felt as if I was deserting him and really grieved when Bob's dad called to ask permission to have him put to sleep as he had developed some paralysis in his back legs. I always felt as if had I been there I could have nursed him back to heath. Funny, the older Stubby my present dog, gets the more he reminds me of Willie. He is now my dearest friend and constant companion. Really don't feel I could have gotten through these past three years without his warm and comforting presence. I wonder if there is such a thing as re-incarnation in the dog world?

Bob had found an awfully nice little house for us. It was just a year old and owned by a Marine captain who had been transferred just after he bought it a year earlier so he had never lived in it but had rented it to another Navy couple who had also just been transferred. Thank goodness the owner happened to be in Kingsville and dropped by a day or so after we moved in. Couldn't believe anyone could so deface a house in such a short time. The floors looked like raw lumber (though under the beds they were shiny and well varnished). The tenants had put large posters all over the walls, affixing them with masking tape. When they moved out, they just ripped the pictures off the wall leaving parts of the tape, but where it pulled off, it took the paper with it. For some obscure reason they removed every lock from every door—the whole mechanism including the latches—so it was impossible to close a door tightly unless you braced something against it—nothing left but gaping holes in the door large enough to stick your fist through. We never could figure out why they did it.

The house had numerous other inhabitants besides us. Outside the front door was a delightful red banana tree, and we

Trying to keep cool in Kingsville, 1945. My outfit was the first of the two-piece bathing suits. Black dotted Swiss and white lace, yet—and no uplift—considered very avant garde in its time.

ate them as they ripened until unfortunately we had another mini-hurricane which blew the tree over. Betty and Al were visiting us at the time, and Betty took all the green bananas home with her. Al said afterward he never ate so many bananas in all his life, she tried every recipe known to man. Under the aforementioned tree was a tarantula's hole. Scared me to death, but he turned out to be quite amenable. We didn't bother him and he didn't bother us.

Inside the house were scorpions. Found one in my bedroom slipper, one running across the floor and a third in the bathtub. We assumed they came in pairs and uneasily shook out shoes and bed clothes and poked in corners all the rest of the time we were there, but never found the fourth one.

Our strangest co-inhabitants, though, were the ants. The kitchen was long and narrow, and mostly white, and every morning around 7:00 a.m. came a long procession of them. Started from one corner of the kitchen and went, a steady line across the floor up to the sink, across it, across the drain board, down to the floor and out through a crack in the bottom of the outside kitchen door. Nothing stopped them in their march, and once they were gone we saw no sign of them until the following morning when they again made their hegira.

The town of Kingsville seemed to be misplaced in time, the sidewalks were for the most part wooden and covered by wooden roofs, which actually was pleasant when you considered that the temperature was over 100 degrees almost every day while we were there.

I really had to take a deep breath to make myself go into the local grocery store, the only things refrigerated were the meat and dairy lockers and the meat counter. Nobody ever seemed to sweep out the store, and if the vegetables were crisp and fresh when put out, the heat quickly wilted them into abject objects.

I tried to go to Corpus to the Commissary once a week and even that, as I've mentioned before, wasn't the greatest. As soon as V.J. day occurred, all rationing was removed, but just because you didn't need red or blue stamps, it didn't mean you could buy all the meat or canned goods you wanted. In fact, it took several years for the shortages to disappear. The local ranchers released what they called beef, but it wasn't really. It hadn't passed the veal stage and was pink instead of red and completely without flavor. All the best produce was sent out of the state, naturally, because they could get better prices. The first fresh orange juice we had was in the airport in New Orleans when Anne and I were on our way back to New England.

The Navy warned us officially to be wary of the drinking water in the area so we used bottled water, but then used to go to the local ice house periodically for shaved ice which I sucked all day long, to keep me cool and un-thirsty, and then wondered why I had to take a dose of Kaopectate automatically every morning.

Kingsville was a dry town. The land was given to the town by the King family whose ranch abutted the town, and since they didn't drink anything alcoholic neither could the townspeople. I almost caused a riot by unthinkingly inquiring in the drug store about a bottle of bitters. Actually, it really bothered us not at all. There was a marvelous wine mess on the air station to which we and all of our friends had access.

Chapter 13

We had a very relaxed six weeks, out last navy tour of duty. It really was quite difficult to realize that the pressure and uncertainty of the last six years had disappeared. Everyone was in the same frame of mind and we partied a lot. There were plenty of dependable WAVE's who enjoyed babysitting with Anne (anything to get in a private home), and we were out more evenings than we were home. In late September Bob learned he had enough points to be released—you got so many points for overseas duty, so many for actual combat, etc. Bob had enough to be one of the first to be separated. Though he retired from active duty after the war, Bob remained a weekend warrior until Korea, when he resigned, feeling he'd really done his share in defense of his country. But the Navy was always important in our lives.

Things Bob thought were funny he'd talk about, like getting lost in a thundercloud when he was a student pilot in Pensacola, landing some place in Alabama and almost getting washed out as a result. Or flying under a bridge in Norfolk just to show off for some little old southern gal; or having the engine of his new F3F fall out of the plane over a cotton patch in Virginia tipping him out at about 400 feet. He got a caterpillar pin (exclusive club of that era for pilots who had to bail out) which he gave to another little old southern gal long before I met him.

Since Bob did most of his flying at night, he developed a strange habit. He said once your eyes were used to it, you could see to drive a car better at night if you drove without lights. Not in traffic, of course, but in the country, off would go the car lights—and it was true. Bob said a curious thing happened to pilots when flying at night over vast stretches of the Pacific. The sky and sea looked so alike, stars, moon, and vagrant clouds seemingly both above and below, that suddenly they couldn't tell whether they were flying right side up or upside down. Fortunately there was an instrument on the panel to tell them which side was up.

Bob had a very salty vocabulary; he seldom made a statement without at least one swear word in it. His mother was horrified; she said he's surely picked it up in the Navy, and as proof produced a Sunday School certificate commending him for not having missed a class in twelve years. However, when I knew him he used all the swearwords from A to Z, and I became so used to them I hardly noticed—but after he was no longer here I found I missed them. Once in a while when I was first alone, and feeling at the bottom of an abyss of loneliness, I'd say a few of his favorites to myself and they evolved into this rather blasphemous litany: Jesus Christ, but this-is-a-goddamn-son-of-a-bitch-of-a-hell-of-a-stinking, frigging, fucking life. Strange and

143

unladylike, but when in utter despair I'd say them, less as time works its healing ways, I found it helped. I guess it was association with happier times when we were young and together and the good life stretched ahead. These four-letter words are the only ones you'll find in this book, though today the popularity of any given book seems to be in direct proportion to the number of its four-letter words and scatalogical phrases. Nor will you find any sex per se; not that there wasn't plenty of it and not that it wasn't perfect. But very private and not for the delectation of a prurient public.

Chapter 14

Bob had to go Jacksonville for the actual separation, and since it was a long and grueling drive from Corpus to Jax and then to East Longmeadow we decided he would take all our stuff, the silver and emergency cruise box and red hat in the car, and Anne and I would go by plane. War priorities were off by then so we were pretty certain of arriving at our destination on time and on the same plane on which we left Corpus. Bob was certain that he wanted to get out of the service, go back to New England and go to work at Springfield Bronze and Aluminum Co. I had some feelings of ambivalence, but it didn't matter; I'd have lived in a tent in the middle of the Sahara or in an igloo on Attu if it meant that, after these tumultuous years, Bob and I could be together for the rest of our lives. I also felt it was really important for Anne to live in her own house for a change, and put down roots. In her short three years she'd been moved some twelve or thirteen times, and after we left Hingham when she was six weeks old, we'd always been in someone else's house sharing it with them, except for Far Rockaway, Wakefield, and Kingsville.

On the other hand, I'd always loved life in the Navy. Having been born and raised in D.C., I grew up with lots of navy juniors—years ago, before aviation came to the forefront, many navy families lived in Washington when the husbands were at sea, and the Navy Department was there too. Most important, the Naval Academy was just a wobble, bounce, and amble way away (local term for the Washington, Baltimore and Annapolis railroad) and nothing was as exciting as navy blue and brass buttons, and going to events at Annapolis.

I really didn't know whether I could cope with life in New England. I'd been brought up in a relaxed southern environment, and pre-war Navy life was of the same ilk. Everyone had maids and housekeeping was at the bottom of the list; living graciously and generally enjoying life were the important things. But from my 4 years in and out of New England I'd gathered that housekeeping was of utmost importance. When Bob's mother entertained her bridge club she'd clean out her bureau drawers because the ladies, when they went to the bathroom, might decide to go exploring anywhere. Even one spot on the kitchen linoleum was a crime. But my desire for a permanent home life with my dearest love outweighed everything else, so in early October Bob put Anne and me on a plane out of Corpus while he headed for Jacksonville and separation.

We had spent the month previous to Anne's birthday, August 31st, teaching her, when asked her age, to hold up three fingers and say, "I'm three years old.", but when we made reservations for the two of us to fly north, we had quickly to debrief her because the cut-off date for small fry to fly for free was three. Fortunately, no one on the flight asked her, and she didn't volunteer the information. I really don't think, though, they would have done anything about it had they found out. The nation was still pretty much in a state of euphoria, and furthermore the miniature pair of Navy wings which Bob had given Anne to wear on her coat opened all doors to her.

We came into LaGuardia around 1:30 a.m., took a limousine into the city and headed for the old Barclay Hotel. The next morning we took the train up to Springfield where Bob's mother and dad met us. Bob drove in one evening about a week later, separated from the Navy actively, but still on the reserve list, and we began the happy task of looking for a permanent home.

Chapter 15

It was strange, during the war whenever Bob came home we all got along very well in his family's house, but now we had a very difficult time, and things grew progressively more uncomfortable so that it was with great deal of relief that we found a nice little house in a pretty little housing development off Island Pond Road in Springfield, and immediately ran into another hitch. Bob hadn't started to work at Springfield Bronze and Aluminum Company as yet, and since he technically had no job, the bank wouldn't give him a loan to buy the house. I think Bob's father was anxious for us to go as we were to get out so he took out the loan for us, and Bob had it transferred as soon as he received his first pay check. And so on November 1, 1945, the moving van came from Boston with all our household goods and chattels which had been in storage since December of 1942, and we moved into our first very own home, the culmination of all our hopes and plans since December 7, 1941. It was so good to see all our furniture again—most particularly the oversized old mahogany sleigh bed which I had inherited from my southern grandmother. I have always been an advocate of the double bed as conducive to a more secure marriage, and yet nine out of ten of the places we could find to live in during the war years were equipped with twin beds—our honeymoon cottage at Warner's, our first little duplex, our house in Wollaston, our attic hideaway in Norfolk, my sister's house in Betheseda, our house on the boulder in Rhode Island and even Betty and Al's guest room in Corpus. Unless we were some place like the last mentioned where the temperature at night cooled off to a steamy 85 degrees we always occupied just one of the available beds which, particularly when we were first married, could be rather embarrassing until we learned to rumple up the other bed. Anyone glancing in the bedroom and seeing the unslept in twin bed was apt to smirk knowingly.

How lovely it was to stretch out luxuriously in our big old double bed and fall asleep with my head on Bob's shoulder knowing that tomorrow and the day after that and the day after that would be the same—no more sudden sad partings or months of waiting alone for I knew not what. Besides it was divine to have a warm body to put my cold feet on after I had had to get up in the middle of the night to tend to Anne's little needs.

I have been penning this epistle for well over a year, reliving each incident as I described it and so I seem to be feeling a great let down as I come to the end. The ending itself seems quite anticlimatic, but I guess that's the way we wanted it to be. As an afterword, poor Bruce is never mentioned because he wasn't there. Wo was the only one who said she'd take me in if I became pregnant during the war. All the rest of the relatives

147

The cherished Alpha and Omega of our war odyssey, circa 1949.

threatened us with ex-communication, and so Bruce was forced to remain the proverbial gleam in his father's eye until we had our own house and a way of life uninterrupted by treks from the east coast to the west coast or from New England to the Mexican border.

Both children were a product of their times. Anne a pre-Pearl Harbor baby and a nomad for her first three years, and Bruce a member of the post-war baby boom who lived in the same house from the time he was born until he left home to go to college and thence into the wide, wide world.

They both came of age during the sixties, but that is their story to tell not mine.

I only know that these six years that I have written about, though they were full of uncertainty, anxiety and even terror at times, were also full of moments of excitement, contentment and great happiness, and they were the cornerstone for a good marriage that would last for the next 37 years until there was no more time for us.

18 May, 1945 At sea

My Darling,

We are on our way back to the states for the last time.

It will be so wonderful to be with you again, and when this war is finally over, we will have every day to ourselves. We'll live and play and work and dream, and all our dreams will come true.

I love you,
Bob

And they did.

Envoi

The year after Bob died, my dear long-time friend, Betty Ferguson, who lives in Coronado—alone now too, invited me to visit her there in the summer. We hadn't seen each other for some thirty years, although we had kept in touch all that time. I planned to stay just a week in case the years had changed us so that we no longer shared the same compatibility we had had in our 1939 penthouse days. We weren't even sure we would recognize each other, but when I walked down the ramp in the San Diego Airport, there she was, her features a little shaded by time, as were mine, but otherwise, it was just as if I were returning to the penthouse from a day's work in San Diego and as if we had never been separated at all. We settled into our easy companionship at once, and so it has been when I return every summer.

It is a very relaxed and peaceful time for me, and I hope for Betty, too. We visit old friends or walk the dog on the beach, or just sit in her lovely flower-enclosed patio, reminiscing about far off times and people.

Back east, no matter what the weather, I walk three or four miles each morning, so I continue the practice out there—walking past all the places that are associated with my memories of Coronado. Although the town has been completely built up, everything is still recognizable—even the bench on the breakwater where Bob and I used to sit and dream.

I always save for the last the little duplex at 959E. It is now green instead of white, and a small house is jammed in on the lawn where we used to practice chip shots, but otherwise it is just the same.

Some years ago I read a very interesting book the name of which I cannot remember, nor can I remember the author, but I loved its premise. It concerned itself with a man who from time to time would find himself removed from present day New York City, to life there in the late nineteenth century, where eventually he decided to remain. No matter when I walk by our honeymoon duplex, the blinds are down, and there is no sign of life, and I always get the feeling that if I went up the stairs and opened the door I would walk right into those lovely months Bob and I had had together there. Once again, we would share all the good times, and (with apologies to Keats) forever would Bob love, and I be fair.

As I am now.

About the Author

I was born Anne Loring Reed in Washington, D.C. on February 5, 1915 and lived there until I went away to college in 1932.

My childhood was uneventful. I was in grade school during the era when if anyone showed a glimmer of intelligence he or she was skipped a grade. As a consequence I finished eight years of grammar school in five and a half years. I was able to keep up mentally and physically but not emotionally with children who were almost three years older than I. I therefore spent a rather lonely several years mitigating the loneliness by reading voraciously anything I could get my hands on.

To counteract this imbalance I then took five years in high school—the last year at Holton Arms, a private school in Washington, where I prepped for the college boards (S.A.T.'s of our era) which would get me into Smith in the fall of 1932.

My one claim to literary accomplishment is that by writing an interesting enough essay on the English college board, I was exempted from freshman English (to the utter disbelief of my English teacher). Our views of literature were diametrically opposed, and she had told me I might as well not take the English exam as I never would pass it.

I majored in English Lit at Smith and did take one course in creative writing, but the only writing I have ever done until *From Sea to Shining Sea and Back Again* was writing letters. I have always loved the feel of a pen in my hand and have deluged friends and relatives with letters ever since I can remember.

In the summer of 1937 I moved to Coronado, California. I went to business school in San Diego while living with my sister and brother-in-law who was a Naval aviator. I subsequently got a job as a social worker for the California State Relief. In October of 1939 I married Robert McCullough, also a Naval aviator and spent the next six years chasing him from California to Massachusetts, to Virginia to Texas and back again, taking time out only to produce our daughter, Anne. For short periods of time I was able to catch up with him.

When the war was finally over, my husband went on Naval reserve status, and we settled in Springfield, Massachusetts.

We lived in our first house in Springfield from November 1945 to March 1947. Bruce was in the offing so we moved to a larger house in Longmeadow (bedroom town for both Springfield, Massachusetts and Hartford, Connecticut). It is now 1992, and everyone else has gone, but I am still here.

We spent the next twenty years as a typical, suburban family. Bob was very outgoing and took part in all sorts of civic enterprises—Junior Chamber of Commerce, Longmeadow Mens' Club, Kiwanis, of which he was president one year and Springfield Boys Club of which he was a member of the board, to mention a few. He later became president of Springfield Bronze and Aluminum Company which made parts for Pratt and Whitney engines many of which are still lying on the surface of the moon.

In 1950 we bought a summer cottage on a lake in West Brookfield, Massachusetts close enough so that Bob could commute to work each day.

Anne went to the University of Massachusetts but left school to get married at the end of her sophomore year. In due time she gave us two delightful grandsons. About three years ago she went back to college and completed the needed courses for her B.A.

Bruce went to the University of New Hampshire and got his Bachelors degree in biology. He then got his Masters in educaton and now teaches science.

In 1966, Bob suddenly discovered he had cancer, and our lives changed completely. He worked for several years, but we both decided we had better make the most of our allotted time so he sold the Springfield Bronze and Aluminum Company and retired—not only from business, but from society in general.

We spent six months at the lake and six months in Longmeadow. We very seldom went out or entertained except our children and grandchildren on occasion. We lived in a very small and secluded world, but it was perfect until time ran out for us on my birthday in 1982.

It was in January of 1983 that Anne, and Bruce asked me to write down my memories of Bob's and my life during the first years: of our marriage and in so doing enabled me to learn to cope with my life as it has become. I never expected it to be anything but a small personal handwritten journal, but like Topsy it seems to have "just growed" into *From Sea to Shining Sea and Back Again* and thence to *Letters from the Far Side of the Shining Sea*.